Richard III

Makers of History Series

Jacob Abbott

PREFACE

King Richard the Third, known commonly in history as Richard the Usurper, was perhaps as bad a man as the principle of hereditary sovereignty ever raised to the throne, or perhaps it should rather be said, as the principle of hereditary sovereignty ever made. There is no evidence that his natural disposition was marked with any peculiar depravity. He was made reckless, unscrupulous, and cruel by the influences which surrounded him, and the circumstances in which he lived, and by being habituated to believe, from his earliest childhood, that the family to which he belonged were born to live in luxury and splendor, and to reign, while the millions that formed the great mass of the community were created only to toil and to obey. The manner in which the principles of pride, ambition, and desperate love of power, which were instilled into his mind in his earliest years, brought forth in the end their legitimate fruits, is clearly seen by the following narrative.

CONTENTS

Chapter I
Richard's Mother

The great quarrel between the houses of York and Lancaster.
Terrible results of the quarrel.
Origin of it.

The mother of King Richard the Third was a beautiful, and, in many respects, a noble-minded woman, though she lived in very rude, turbulent, and trying times. She was born, so to speak, into one of the most widely-extended, the most bitter, and the most fatal of the family quarrels which have darkened the annals of the great in the whole history of mankind, namely, that long-protracted and bitter contest which was waged for so many years between the two great branches of the family of Edward the Third—the houses of York and Lancaster—for the possession of the kingdom of England. This dreadful quarrel lasted for more than a hundred years. It led to wars and commotions, to the sacking and burning of towns, to the ravaging of fruitful countries, and to atrocious deeds of violence of every sort, almost without number. The internal peace of hundreds of thousands of families all over the land was destroyed by it for many generations. Husbands were alienated from wives, and parents from children by it. Murders and assassinations innumerable grew out of it. And what was it all about? you will ask. It arose from the fact that the descendants of a certain king had married and intermarried among each other in such a complicated manner that for several generations nobody could tell which of two different lines of candidates was fairly entitled to the throne. The question was settled at last by a prince who inherited the claim on one side marrying a princess who was the heir on the other. Thus the conflicting interests of the two houses were combined, and the quarrel was ended.

But, while the question was pending, it kept the country in a state of perpetual commotion, with feuds, and quarrels, and combats innumerable, and all the other countless and indescribable horrors of civil war.

Intricate questions of genealogy and descent.

The two branches of the royal family which were engaged in this quarrel were called the houses of York and Lancaster, from the fact that those were the titles of the fathers and heads of the two lines respectively. The Lancaster party were the descendants of John of Gaunt, Duke of Lancaster, and the York party were the successors and heirs of his brother Edmund, Duke of York. These men were both sons of Edward the Third, the King of England who reigned immediately before Richard the Second. A full account of the family is given in our history of Richard the Second. Of course, they being brothers, their children were cousins, and they ought to have lived together in peace and harmony. And then, besides being related to each other through their fathers, the two branches of the family intermarried together, so as to make the relationships in the following generations so close and so complicated that it was almost impossible to disentangle them. In reading the history of those times, we find dukes or princes fighting each other in the field, or laying plans to assassinate each other, or striving to see which should make the other a captive, and shut him up in a dungeon for the rest of his days; and yet these enemies, so exasperated and implacable, are very near relations—cousins, perhaps, if the relationship is reckoned in one way, and uncle and nephew if it is reckoned in another. During the period of this struggle, all the great personages of the court, and all, or nearly all, the private families of the kingdom, and all the towns and the villages, were divided and distracted by the dreadful feud.

SCENES OF CIVIL WAR

Lady Cecily Neville.

Richard's mother, whose name, before she was married, was Lady

Cecily Neville, was born into one side of this quarrel, and then afterward married into the other side of it. This is a specimen of the way in which the contest became complicated in multitudes of cases. Lady Cecily was descended from the Duke of Lancaster, but she married the Duke of York, in the third generation from the time when the quarrel began.

She becomes Duchess of York.
Her mode of life.

Of course, upon her marriage, Lady Cecily Neville became the Duchess of York. Her husband was a man of great political importance in his day, and, like the other nobles of the land, was employed continually in wars and in expeditions of various kinds, in the course of which he was continually changing his residence from castle to castle all over England, and sometimes making excursions into Ireland, Scotland, and France. His wife accompanied him in many of these wanderings, and she led, of course, so far as external circumstances were concerned, a wild and adventurous life. She was, however, very quiet and domestic in her tastes, though proud and ambitious in her aspirations, and she occupied herself, wherever she was, in regulating her husband's household, teaching and training her children, and in attending with great regularity and faithfulness to her religious duty, as religious duty was understood in those days.

The following is an account, copied from an ancient record, of the manner in which she spent her days at one of the castles where she was residing.

> Extract from the ancient annals.
>
> "She useth to arise at seven of the clock, and hath readye her chapleyne to say with her mattins of the daye (that is, morning prayers), and when she is fully readye, she hath a lowe mass in her chamber. After mass she taketh something to recreate nature, and soe goeth to the chapelle, hearinge the divine service and two lowe masses. From thence to dynner, during the tyme of whih she hath a lecture of holy matter (that is, reading from a religious book), either Hilton of Contemplative and Active Life, or some other spiritual and instructive work. After dynner she giveth audyence to all such as hath any matter to shrive unto her, by the space of one hower, and then sleepeth one quarter of an hower, and

3

after she hath slept she contynueth in prayer until the first peale of even songe.

"In the tyme of supper she reciteth the lecture that was had at dynner to those that be in her presence. After supper she disposeth herself to be famyliare with her gentlewomen to the seasoning of honest myrthe, and one hower before her going to bed she taketh a cup of wine, and after that goeth to her pryvie closette, and taketh her leave of God for all nighte, makinge end of her prayers for that daye, and by eighte of the clocke is in bedde."

The going to bed at eight o'clock was in keeping with the other arrangements of the day, for we find by a record of the rules and orders of the duchess's household that the dinner-hour was eleven, and the supper was at four.

Lady Cecily's family.
Names of the children.

This lady, Richard's mother, during her married life, had no less than twelve children. Their names were Anne, Henry, Edward, Edmund, Elizabeth, Margaret, William, John, George, Thomas, Richard, and Ursula. Thus Richard, the subject of this volume, was the eleventh, that is, the last but one. A great many of these, Richard's brothers and sisters, died while they were children. All the boys died thus except four, namely, Edward, Edmund, George, and Richard. Of course, it is only with those four that we have any thing to do in the present narrative.

The boys' situation and mode of life.
Their letters.

Several of the other children, however, besides these three, lived for some time. They resided generally with their mother while they were young, but as they grew up they were often separated both from her and from their father—the duke, their father, being often called away from home, in the course of the various wars in which he was engaged, and his wife frequently accompanied him. On such occasions the boys were left at some castle or other, under the care of persons employed to take charge of their education. They used to write letters to their father from time to time, and it is curious that these letters are the earliest examples of letters from children to parents which have been preserved in history. Two of the boys were at one time under the charge of a man named Richard Croft, and the boys thought that he was too strict with them. One of the letters, which has been preserved, was written to complain of this strictness, or, as the boy expressed it, "the odieux rule and demeaning" of their tutor, and also to ask for some "fyne bonnets," which the writer wished to have sent for himself and for his little brother. There is another long letter extant which was written at nearly the same time. This letter was written, or at least signed, by two of the boys, Edward and Edmund, and was addressed to their father on the occasion of some of his victories. But, though signed by the boys' names, I suspect, from the lofty language in which it is expressed, and from the many high-flown expressions of duty which it contains, that it was really written *for* the boys by their mother or by one of their teachers. Of this, however, the reader can judge for himself on perusing the letter. In this copy the spelling is modernized so as to make it more intelligible, but the language is transcribed exactly from the original.

Letter written by Edward and Edmund.

"Right high and mighty prince, our most worshipful and greatly redoubted lord and father:

"In as lowly a wise as any sons can or may, we recommend us unto your good lordship, and please it to your highness to wit, that we have received your worshipful letters yesterday by your servant William Clinton, bearing date at York, the 29th day of May. [1]

The boys congratulate their father on his victories.

"By the which William, and by the relation of John Milewater, we conceive your worshipful and victorious speed against your enemies, to their great shame, and to us the most comfortable things that we desire to hear. Whereof we thank Almighty God of his gifts, beseeching him heartily to give you that good and cotidian[2] fortune hereafter to know your enemies, and to have the victory over them.

"And if it please your highness to know of our welfare, at the making of this letter we were in good health of body,

---

[1] There were no postal arrangements in those days, and all letters were sent by private, and generally by special messengers.
[2] Daily.

thanked be God, beseeching your good and gracious fatherhood for our daily blessing.

"And whereas you command us by your said letters to attend specially to our learning in our young age, that should cause us to grow to honor and worship in our old age, please it your highness to wit, that we have attended to our learning since we came hither, and shall hereafter, by the which we trust to God your gracious lordship and good fatherhood shall be pleased.

"Also we beseech your good lordship that it may please you to send us Harry Lovedeyne, groom of your kitchen, whose service is to us right agreeable; and we will send you John Boyes to wait upon your lordship.

"Right high and mighty prince, our most worshipful and greatly redoubted lord and father, we beseech Almighty God to give you as good life and long as your own princely heart can best desire.

"Written at your Castle of Ludlow, the 3d of June.

"Your humble sons,
"E. Marche.
"E. Rutland."

Further particulars about the boys.

The subscriptions E. March and E. Rutland stand for Edward, Earl of March, and Edmund, Earl of Rutland; for, though these boys were then only eleven and twelve years of age respectively, they were both earls. One of them, afterward, when he was about seventeen years old, was cruelly killed on the field of battle, where he had been fighting with his father, as we shall see in another chapter. The other, Edward, became King of England. He came immediately before Richard the Third in the line.

The letter which the boys wrote was superscribed as follows:

"To the right high and mighty prince, our most worshipful and greatly redoubted lord and father, the Duke of York, Protector and Defender of England."

LUDLOW CASTLE

Character of Richard's mother.

Lady Cecily, as we have already seen, was in many respects a noble woman, and a most faithful and devoted wife and mother; she was, however, of a very lofty and ambitious spirit, and extremely proud of her rank and station. Almost all her brothers and sisters—and the family was very large—were peers and peeresses, and when she married Prince Richard Plantagenet, her heart beat high with exultation and joy to think that she was about to become a queen. She believed that Prince Richard was fully entitled to the throne at that time, for reasons which will be fully explained in the next chapter, and that, even if his claims should not be recognized until the death of the king who was then reigning, they certainly would be so recognized then, and she would become an acknowledged queen, as she thought she was already one by right. So she felt greatly exalted in spirit, and moved and acted among all who surrounded her with an air of stately reserve of the most grand and aristocratic character.

CASTLE AND PARK OF THE MIDDLE AGES

In fact, there has, perhaps, no time and place been known in the history of the world in which the spirit of aristocracy was more lofty and overbearing in its character than in England during the period when the Plantagenet family were in prosperity and power. The nobles formed then, far more strikingly than they do now, an entirely distinct and exalted class, that looked down upon all other ranks and gradations of society as infinitely beneath them. Their only occupation was war, and they regarded all those who were engaged in any employments whatever, that were connected with art or industry, with utter disdain. These last were crowded together in villages and towns which were formed of dark and narrow streets, and rude and comfortless dwellings. The nobles lived in grand castles scattered here and there over the country, with extensive parks and pleasure-grounds around them, where they loved to marshal their followers, and inaugurate marauding expeditions against their rivals or their enemies. They were engaged in constant wars and contentions with each other, each thirsting for more power and more splendor than he at present enjoyed, and treating all beneath him with the utmost haughtiness and disdain. Richard's mother exhibited this aristocratic loftiness of spirit in a very high degree, and it was undoubtedly in a great manner through the influence which she exerted over her children that they were inspired with those sentiments of ambition and love of glory to which the crimes and miseries into which several of them fell in their subsequent career were owing.

To assist her in the early education of her children, Richard's mother appointed one of the ladies of the court their governess. This governess was a personage of very high rank, being descended from the royal line. With the ideas which Lady Cecily entertained of the exalted position of her family, and of the future destiny of her children, none but a lady of high rank would be thought worthy of being intrusted with such a charge. The name of the governess was Lady Mortimer.

The boys, as they grew older, were placed under the charge of a governor. His name was Sir Richard Croft. It is this Sir Richard that they allude to in their letter. He, too, was a person of high rank and of great military distinction. The boys, however, thought him too strict and severe with them; at least so it would seem, from the manner in which they speak of him in the letter.

The governor and the governess appear to have liked each other very well, for after a time Sir Richard offered himself to Lady Mortimer, and they were married.

Besides Ludlow Castle, Prince Richard had several other strongholds, where his wife from time to time resided. Richard, who was one of the youngest of the children, was born at one of these, called Fotheringay Castle; but, before coming to the event of his birth, I must give some account of the history and fortunes of his father.

Chapter II
Richard's Father
A.D. 1415-1461

Genealogy of Richard Plantagenet.
Family of Edward III.

Richard's father was a prince of the house of York. In the course of his life he was declared heir to the crown, but he died before he attained possession of it, thus leaving it for his children. The nature of his claim to the crown, and, indeed, the general relation of the various branches of the family to each other, will be seen by the genealogical table on the next page but one.

Edward the Third, who reigned more than one hundred years before Richard the Third, and his queen Philippa, left at their decease four sons, as appears by the table. They had other children besides these, but it was only these four, namely, Edward, Lionel, John, and Edmund, whose descendants were involved in the quarrels for the succession. The others either died young, or else, if they arrived at maturity, the lines descending from them soon became extinct.

Succession of heirs in the family of Edward III.

Of the four that survived, the oldest was Edward, called in history the Black Prince. A full account of his life and adventures is given in our history of Richard the Second. He died before his father, and so did not attain to the crown. He, however, left his son Richard his heir, and at Edward's death Richard became king. Richard reigned twenty years, and then, in consequence of his numerous vices and crimes, and of his general mismanagement, he was deposed, and Henry, the son of John of Gaunt, Duke of Lancaster, Edward's third son, ascended the throne in his stead.

Union of the houses of Clarence and York.

Still, though the people of England generally acquiesced in this, the families of the other brothers, namely, of Lionel and Edmund, called generally the houses of Clarence and of York, were not satisfied. They combined together, and formed a great many plots and conspiracies against the house of Lancaster, and many insurrections and wars, and many cruel deeds of violence and murder grew out of the quarrel. At length, to strengthen their alliance more fully, Richard, the second son of Edmund of York, married Anne, a descendant of the Clarence line. The other children, who came before these, in the two lines, soon afterward died, leaving the inheritance of both to this pair. Their son was Richard, the father of Richard the Third. He is called Richard Plantagenet, Duke of York. On the death of his father and mother, he, of course, became the heir not only of the immense estates and baronial rights of both the lines from which he had descended, but also of the claims of the older line to the crown of England.

The successive generations of these three lines, down to the period of the union of the second and fourth, cutting off the third, is shown clearly in the table.

GENEALOGICAL TABLE OF THE FAMILY OF EDWARD III.,
SHOWING THE CONNECTION OF
THE HOUSES OF YORK AND LANCASTER

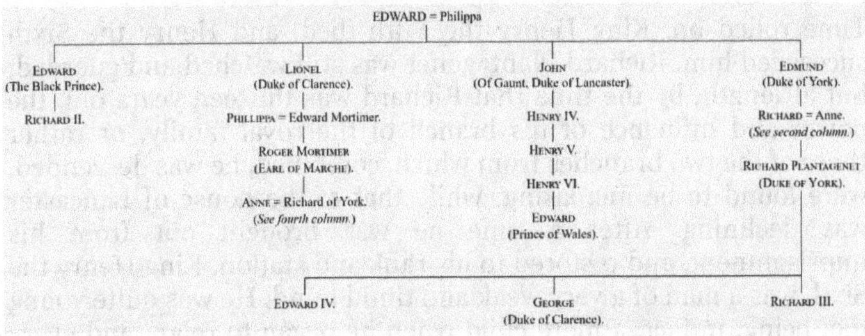

The character = denotes marriage; the short perpendicular line | a descent. There were many other children and descendants in the different branches of the family besides those whose names are inserted in the table. The table includes only those essential to an understanding of the history.

Now, as appears by the table, John of Gaunt was the third of the four sons, Lionel, Duke of Clarence, being the second. The descendants of Lionel would properly have come before those of John in the succession, but it happened that the only descendants of Lionel were Philippa, a daughter, and Roger, a grandchild, who was at this time an infant. Neither of these were able to assert their claims, although in theory their claims were acknowledged to be prior to those of the descendants of John. The people of England, however, were so desirous to be rid of Richard, that they were willing to submit to the reign of any member of the royal family who should prove strong enough to dispossess him. So they accepted Henry of Lancaster, who ascended the throne as Henry the Fourth, and he and his successors in the Lancastrian line, Henry the Fifth and Henry the Sixth, held the throne for many years.

Richard Plantagenet a prisoner.

Of course, the Lancaster line were much alarmed at the combination of the claims of their rivals. King Henry the Fifth was at that period on the throne, and, by the time that Richard Plantagenet was three years old, under pretense of protecting him from danger, he caused him to be shut up in a castle, and kept a close prisoner there.

King Henry VI.
His gentle and quiet character.
Portrait.

Time rolled on. King Henry the Fifth died, and Henry the Sixth succeeded him. Richard Plantagenet was still watched and guarded; but at length, by the time that Richard was thirteen years old, the power and influence of his branch of the royal family, or rather those of the two branches from which, combined, he was descended, were found to be increasing, while that of the house of Lancaster was declining. After a time he was brought out from his imprisonment, and restored to his rank and station. King Henry the Sixth was a man of a very weak and timid mind. He was quite young too, being, in fact, a mere child when he began to reign, and every thing went wrong with his government. While he was young, he could, of course, do nothing, and when he grew older he was too gentle and forbearing to control the rough and turbulent spirits around him. He had no taste for war and bloodshed, but loved retirement and seclusion, and, as he advanced in years, he fell into the habit of spending a great deal of his time in acts of piety and devotion, performed according to the ideas and customs of the times. The annexed engraving, representing him as he appeared when he was a boy, is copied from the ancient portraits, and well expresses the mild and gentle traits which marked his disposition and character.

Such being the disposition and character of Henry, every thing during his reign went wrong, and this state of things, growing worse and worse as he advanced in life, greatly encouraged and strengthened the house of York in the effort which they were inclined to make to bring their own branch of the family to the throne.

HENRY VI. IN HIS CHILDHOOD

Discontent of the people.

"See," said they, "what we come to by allowing a line of usurpers to reign. These Henrys of Lancaster are all descended from a younger son, while the heirs of the older are living, and have a right to the throne. Richard Plantagenet is the true and proper heir. He is a man of energy. Let us make him king."

Arrangements made for the succession.

But the people of England, though they gradually came to desire the change, were not willing yet to plunge the country again into a state of civil war for the purpose of making it. They would not disturb Henry, they said, while he continued to live; but there was nobody to succeed him, and, when he died, Richard Plantagenet should be king.

Character of Margaret of Anjou.
No children.
Henry was married at this time, but he had no children. The name of his wife was Margaret of Anjou. She was a very extraordinary and

13

celebrated woman. Though very beautiful in person, she was as energetic and masculine in character as her poor husband was effeminate and weak, and she took every thing into her own hands. This, however, made matters worse instead of better, and the whole country seemed to rejoice that she had no children, for thus, on the death of Henry, the line would become extinct, and Richard Plantagenet and his descendants would succeed, as a matter of course, in a quiet and peaceful manner. As Henry and Margaret had now been married eight or nine years without any children, it was supposed that they never would have any.

QUEEN MARGARET OF ANJOU, WIFE OF HENRY VI.

Feeble and failing capacity of the king.

Accordingly, Richard Plantagenet was universally looked upon as Henry's successor, and the time seemed to be drawing nigh when the change of dynasty was to take place. Henry's health was very feeble. He seemed to be rapidly declining. His mind was affected, too, quite seriously, and he sometimes sank into a species of torpor from which nothing could arouse him.

Indeed, it became difficult to carry on the government in his name, for the king sank at last into such a state of imbecility that it was impossible to obtain from him the least sign or token that would serve, even for form's sake, as an assent on his part to the royal decrees. At one time Parliament appointed a commission to visit him in his chamber, for the purpose of ascertaining the state that he was in, and to see also whether they could not get some token from him which they could consider as his assent to certain measures which it was deemed important to take; but they could not get from the king any answer or sign of any kind, notwithstanding all that they could do or say. They retired for a time, and afterward came back again to make a second attempt, and then, as an ancient narrative records the story, "they moved and stirred him by all the ways and means that they could think of to have an answer of the said matter, but they could have no answer, word nor sign, and therefore, with sorrowful hearts, came away."

Richard Plantagenet formally declared the heir.

This being the state of things, Parliament thought it time to make some definite arrangements for the succession. Accordingly, they passed a formal and solemn enactment declaring Richard Plantagenet heir presumptive of the crown, and investing him with the rank and privileges pertaining to that position. They also appointed him, for the present, Protector and defender of the realm.

Richard, the subject of this volume, was at this time an infant two years old. The other ten children had been born at various periods before.

Unexpected birth of a prince.
Suspicions.

It was now, of course, expected that Henry would soon die, and that then Richard Plantagenet would at once ascend the throne, acknowledged by the whole realm as the sole and rightful heir. But these expectations were suddenly disturbed, and the whole kingdom was thrown into a state of great excitement and alarm by the news of a very unexpected and important event which occurred at this time, namely, the birth of a child to Margaret, the queen. This event awakened all the latent fires of civil dissension and discord anew. The Lancastrian party, of course, at once rallied around the infant prince, who, they claimed, was the rightful heir to the crown. They began at once to reconstruct and strengthen their plans, and to shape their measures with a view to retain the kingdom in the Lancaster line. On the other hand, the friends of the combined houses of Clarence and York declared that they would not acknowledge the new-comer as the rightful heir. They did not believe that he was the son of the king, for he, as they said, had been for a long time as good as dead. Some said that they did not even believe that the child was Margaret's son. There was a story that she had had a child, but that he was very weak and puny, and that he had died soon after his birth, and that Margaret had cunningly substituted another child in his place, in order to retain her position and power by having a supposed son of hers reign as king after her husband should die. Margaret was a woman of so ambitious and unscrupulous a character, that she was generally believed capable of adopting any measures, however criminal and bold, to accomplish her ends.

Various plans and speculations.
Richard's hopes.

But, notwithstanding these rumors, Parliament acknowledged the infant as his father's son and heir. He was named Edward, and created at once Prince of Wales, which act was a solemn acknowledgment of his right to the succession. Prince Richard made no open opposition to this; for, although he and his friends maintained that he had a right to the crown, they thought that the time had not yet come for openly advancing their claim, so for the present they determined to be quiet. The child might not survive, and his father, the king, being in so helpless and precarious a condition, might cease to live at any time; and if it should so happen that both the father and the child should die, Richard would, of course, succeed at once, without any question. He accordingly thought it best to wait a little while, and see what turn things would take.

He soon found that things were taking the wrong turn. The child lived, and appeared likely to continue to live, and, what was perhaps worse for him, the king, instead of declining more and more, began to revive. In a short time he was able to attend to business again, at least so far as to express his assent to measures prepared for him by his ministers. Prince Richard was accordingly called upon to resign his protectorate. He thought it best to yield to this proposal, and he did so, and thus the government was once more in Henry's hands.

Progress of the formation of parties.

Things went on in this way for two or three years, but the breach between the two great parties was all the time widening. Difficulties multiplied in number and increased in magnitude. The country took sides. Armed forces were organized on one side and on the other, and at length Prince Richard openly claimed the crown as his right. This led to a long and violent discussion in Parliament. The result was, that a majority was obtained to vote in favor of Prince Richard's right. The Parliament decreed, however, that the existing state of things should not be disturbed so long as Henry continued to live, but that at Henry's death the crown should descend, not to little Edward his son, the infant Prince of Wales, but to Prince Richard Plantagenet and his descendants forever.

Queen Margaret's resolution and energy.
Wars.

Queen Margaret was at this time at a castle in Wales, where she had gone with the child, in order to keep him in a place of safety while these stormy discussions were pending. When she heard that Parliament had passed a law setting aside the claims of her child, she declared that she would never submit to it. She immediately sent messengers all over the northern part of the kingdom, summoning the faithful followers of the king every where to arm themselves and assemble near the frontier. She herself went to Scotland to ask for aid. The King of Scotland at that time was a child, but he was related to the Lancastrian family, his grandmother having been a descendant of John of Gaunt, the head of the Lancaster line. He was too young to take any part in the war, but his mother, who was acting as regent, furnished Margaret with troops. Margaret, putting herself at the head of these forces, marched across the frontier into England, and joined herself there to the other forces which had assembled in answer to her summons.

Richard's two brothers, Edward and Edmund.

In the mean time, Prince Richard had assembled his adherents too, and had commenced his march to the northward to meet his enemies. He took his two oldest sons with him, the two that wrote the letter quoted in the last chapter. One of these you will recollect was Edward, Earl of Marche, and the second was Edmund, Earl of Rutland. Edward was now about eighteen years of age, and his brother Edmund about seventeen. One would have said that at this period of life they were altogether too young to be exposed to the hardships, fatigues, and dangers of a martial campaign; but it was the custom in those times for princes and nobles to be taken with their fathers to fields of battle at a very early age. And these youthful warriors were really of great service too, for the interest which they inspired among all ranks of the army was so great, especially when their rank was very high, that they were often the means of greatly increasing the numbers and the enthusiasm of their fathers' followers.

Edward, indeed, was in this instance deemed old enough to be sent off on an independent service, and so, while the prince moved forward with the main body of his army toward the north, he dispatched Edward, accompanied by a suitable escort, to the westward, toward the frontiers of Wales, to assemble all the armed men that he could find in that part of the kingdom who were disposed to espouse his cause. Edmund, who was a year younger than Edward, went with his father.

The walls of York.

The prince proceeded to the city of York, which was then a fortified place of great strength. The engraving gives a very good idea of the appearance of the walls in those times. These walls remain, indeed, almost entire at the present day, and they are visited a great deal by tourists and travelers, being regarded with much interest as furnishing a very complete and well-preserved specimen of the mural fortifications of the Middle Ages. Such walls, however, would be almost entirely useless now as means of defense, since they would not stand at all against an attack from modern artillery.

The great church seen over the walls, in the heart of the city, is the famous York minster, one of the grandest Cathedral churches in England. It was a hundred and fifty years in building, and it was completed about two centuries before Richard's day.

Prince Richard at York.

When Prince Richard reached York, he entered the town, and established himself there, with a view of waiting till his son should arrive with the re-enforcements which he had been sent to seek in the western part of England.

Boldness of the queen.

While he was there, and before the re-enforcements came, the queen, at the head of her army from Scotland, which was strengthened, moreover, by the troops which she had obtained in the north of England, came marching on down the country in great force. When she came into the neighborhood of York, she encamped, and then sent messengers to Prince Richard, taunting and deriding him for having shut himself up within fortified walls, and daring him to come out into the open field and fight her.

WALLS OF YORK

The advice of Richard's counselors.

The prince's counselors advised him to do no such thing. One of them in particular, a certain Sir Davy Hall, who was an old and faithful officer in the prince's service, urged him to pay no attention to Queen Margaret's taunts.

"We are not strong enough yet," said he, "to meet the army which she has assembled. We must wait till our re-enforcements come. By going out now we shall put our cause in great peril, and all to no purpose whatever."

Richard's reply.

"Ah! Davy, Davy," said the prince, "hast thou loved me so long, and now wouldst thou have me dishonored? When I was regent in Normandy, thou never sawest me keep fortress, even when the dauphin himself, with all his power, came to besiege me. [3] I always, like a man, came forth to meet him, instead of remaining within my walls, like a bird shut up in a cage. Now if I did not then keep myself shut up for fear of a great, strong prince, do you think I will now, for

---

[3] In former years Prince Richard had acted as viceroy of the English possessions in France, under King Henry, and while there he had been engaged in wars with the King of France, and with the dauphin, his son.

dread of a scolding woman, whose weapons are only her tongue and her nails, and thus give people occasion to say that I turned dastard before a woman, when no man had ever been able to make me fear? No, I will never submit to such disgrace. I would rather die in honor than live in shame; and so the great numbers of our enemies do not deter me in the least; they rather encourage me; therefore, in the name of God and St. George, advance my banner, for I am determined that I will go out and fight them, if I go alone."

LAST HOURS OF KING RICHARD'S FATHER

The battle.
Richard defeated.
Death of Edmund.

So Prince Richard came forth from the gates of York at the head of his columns, and rode on toward the queen's camp. Edmund went with him. Edmund was under the care of his tutor, Robert Aspell, who was charged to keep close to his side, and to watch over him in the most vigilant manner. The army of the queen was at some distance from York, at a place called Wakefield. Both parties, as is usual in civil wars, were extremely exasperated against each other, and the battle was desperately fought. It was very brief, however, and Richard's troops were defeated. Richard himself was taken prisoner. Edmund endeavored to escape. His tutor endeavored to hurry him off the field, but he was stopped on the way by a certain nobleman of the queen's party, named Lord Clifford. The poor boy begged hard for mercy, but Clifford killed him on the spot.

The prince's army, when they found that the battle had gone against them, and that their captain was a prisoner, fled in all directions over the surrounding country, leaving great numbers dead upon the field. The prince himself, as soon as he was taken, was disarmed on the field, and all the leaders of the queen's army, including, as the most authentic accounts relate, the queen herself, gathered around him in wild exultation. They carried him to a mound formed by an ant-hill, which they said, in mockery, should be his throne. They placed him upon it with taunts and derision. They made a crown for him of knotted grass, and put it upon his head, and then made mock obeisances before him, saying, "Hail! king without a kingdom. Hail! prince without a people."

Death of Richard.
The head set upon a pole at York.

After having satisfied themselves with their taunts and revilings, the party killed their prisoner and cut off his head. They set his head upon the point of a lance, and in this way presented it to Queen Margaret. The queen ordered the head to be decorated with a paper crown, and then to be carried to York, and set up at the gates of that city upon a tall pole.

Thus was little Richard, the subject of this narrative, left fatherless. He was at this period between eight and nine years old.

Chapter III
The Childhood of Richard III

Condition of young Richard in his childhood.

Young Richard, as was said at the close of the last chapter, was of a very tender age when his father and his brother Edmund were killed at the battle of Wakefield. He was at that time only about eight years old. It is very evident too, from what has been already related of the history of his father and mother, that during the whole period of his childhood and youth he must have passed through very stormy times. It is only a small portion of the life of excitement, conflict, and alarm which was led by his father that there is space to describe in this volume. So unsettled and wandering a life did his father and mother lead, that it is not quite certain in which of the various towns and castles that from time to time they made their residence, he was born. It is supposed, however, that he was born in the Castle of Fotheringay, in the year 1452. His father was killed in 1461, which would make Richard, as has already been said, about eight or nine years old at that time.

Strange tales in respect to his birth.

There were a great many strange tales related in subsequent years in respect to Richard's birth. He became such a monster, morally, when he grew to be a man, that the people believed that he was born a monster in person. The story was that he came into the world very ugly in face and distorted in form, and that his hair and his teeth were already grown. These were considered as portents of the ferociousness of temper and character which he was subsequently to manifest, and of the unnatural and cruel crimes which he would live to commit. It is very doubtful, however, whether any of these stories are true. It is most probable that at his birth he looked like any other child.

There were a great many periods of intense excitement and terror in the family history before the great final calamity at Wakefield when Richard's father and his brother Edmund were killed. At these times the sole reliance of the prince in respect to the care of the younger children was upon Lady Cecily, their mother. The older sons went with their father on the various martial expeditions in which he was engaged. They shared with him the hardships and dangers of his conflicts, and the triumph and exultations of his victories. The younger children, however, remained in seclusion with their mother, sometimes in one place and sometimes in another, wherever there was, for the time being, the greatest promise of security.

Dangers to which Richard was exposed in his childhood. Extraordinary vicissitudes in the life of his mother.

Indeed, during the early childhood of Richard, the changes and vicissitudes through which the family passed were so sudden and violent in their character as sometimes to surpass the most romantic tales of fiction. At one time, while Lady Cecily was residing at the Castle of Ludlow with Richard and some of the younger children, a party of her husband's enemies, the Lancastrians, appeared suddenly at the gates of the town, and, before Prince Richard's party had time to take any efficient measures for defense, the town and the castle were both taken. The Lancastrians had expected to find Prince Richard himself in the castle, but he was not there. They were exasperated by their disappointment, and in their fury they proceeded to ransack all the rooms, and to destroy every thing that came into their hands. In some of the inner and more private apartments they found Lady Cecily and her children. They immediately seized them all, made them prisoners, and carried them away. By King Henry's orders, they were placed in close custody in another castle in the southern part of England, and all the property, both of the prince and of Lady Cecily, was confiscated. While the mother and the younger children were thus closely shut up and reduced to helpless destitution, the father and the older sons were obliged to fly from the country to save their lives. In less than three months after this time these same exiled and apparently ruined fugitives were marching triumphantly through the country, at the head of victorious troops, carrying all before them. Lady Cecily and her children were set at liberty, and restored to their property and their rights, while King Henry himself, whose captives they had been, was himself made captive, and brought in durance to London, and Queen Margaret and her son were in their turn compelled to fly from the realm to save their lives.

This last change in the condition of public affairs took place only a short time before the great final contest between Prince Richard of York, King Richard's father, and the family of Henry, when the prince lost his life at Wakefield, as described in the last chapter.

PALACE AND GARDEN BELONGING TO THE HOUSE OF YORK

Of course, young Richard, being brought up amid these scenes of wild commotion, and accustomed from childhood to witness the most cruel and remorseless conflicts between branches of the same family, was trained by them to be ambitious, daring, and unscrupulous in respect to the means to be used in circumventing or destroying an enemy. The seed thus sown produced in subsequent years most dreadful fruit, as will be seen more fully in the sequel of his history.

The castles and palaces belonging to the house of York.

There were a great many hereditary castles belonging to the family of York, many of which had descended from father to son for many generations. Some of these castles were strong fortresses, built in wild and inaccessible retreats, and intended to be used as places of temporary refuge, or as the rallying-points and rendezvous of bodies of armed men. Others were better adapted for the purposes of a private residence, being built with some degree of reference to the comfort of the inmates, and surrounded with gardens and grounds, where the ladies and the children who were left in them could find recreation and amusement adapted to their age and sex.

Situation of Lady Cecily at the time of her husband's death.

It was in such a castle as this, near London, that Lady Cecily and her younger children were residing when her husband went to the northward to meet the forces of the queen, as related in the last chapter. Here Lady Cecily lived in great state, for she thought the time was drawing nigh when her husband would be raised to the throne. Indeed, she considered him as already the true and rightful sovereign of the realm, and she believed that the hour would very soon come when his claims would be universally acknowledged, and when she herself would be Queen of England, and her boys royal princes, and, as such, the objects of universal attention and regard. She instilled these ideas continually into the minds of the children, and she exacted the utmost degree of subserviency and submission toward herself and toward them on the part of all around her.

While she was thus situated in her palace near London, awaiting every day the arrival of a messenger from the north announcing the final victory of her husband over all his foes, she was one day thunderstruck, and overwhelmed with grief and despair, by the tidings that her husband had been defeated, and that he himself, and the dear son who had accompanied him, and was just arriving at maturity, had been ignominiously slain. The queen, too, her most bitter foe, now exultant and victorious, was advancing triumphantly toward London.

Lady Cecily sends the children to the Continent.

Not a moment was to be lost. Lady Cecily had with her, at this time, her two youngest sons, George and Richard. She made immediate arrangements for her flight. It happened that the Earl of Warwick, who was at this time the Lord High Admiral, and who, of course, had command of the seas between England and the Continent, was a relative and friend of Lady Cecily's. He was at this time in London. Lady Cecily applied to him to assist her in making her escape. He consented, and, with his aid, she herself, with her two children and a small number of attendants, escaped secretly from London, and made their way to the southern coast. There Lady Cecily put the children and the attendants on board a vessel, by which they were conveyed to the coast of Holland. On landing there, they were received by the prince of the country, who was a friend of Lady Cecily, and to whose care she commended them. The prince received them with great kindness, and sent them to the city of Utrecht, where he established them safely in one of his palaces, and appointed suitable tutors and governors to superintend their education. Here it was expected that they would remain for several years.

Their mother did not go with them to Holland. Her fears in respect to remaining in England were not for herself, but only for her helpless children. For herself, her only impulse was to face and brave the dangers which threatened her, and triumph over them. So she went boldly back to London, to await there whatever might occur.

Situation of Lady Cecily and of her oldest son.

Besides, her oldest son was still in England, and she could not forsake him. You will recollect that, when his father went north to meet the forces of Queen Margaret, he sent his oldest son, Edward, Earl of Marche, to the western part of England, to obtain re-enforcements. Edward was at Gloucester when the tidings came to him of his father's death. Gloucester is on the western confines of England, near the southeastern borders of Wales. Now, of course, since her husband was dead, all Lady Cecily's ambition, and all her hopes of revenge were concentrated in him. She wished to be at hand to counsel him, and to co-operate with him by all the means in her power. How she succeeded in these plans, and how, by means of them, he soon became King of England, will appear in the next chapter.

Chapter IV

Accession of Edward IV., Richard's elder Brother

A.D. 1461

Edward now becomes heir to the crown.

Richard's brother Edward, as has already been remarked, was at Gloucester when he heard the news of his father's death. This news, of course, made a great change in his condition. To his mother, the event was purely and simply a calamity, and it could awaken no feelings in her heart but those of sorrow and chagrin. In Edward's mind, on the other hand, the first emotions of astonishment and grief were followed immediately by a burst of exultation and pride. He, of course, as now the oldest surviving son, succeeded at once to all the rights and titles which his father had enjoyed, and among these, according to the ideas which his mother had instilled into his mind, was the right to the crown. His heart, therefore, when the first feeling of grief for the loss of his father had subsided, bounded with joy as he exclaimed,

"So now *I* am the King of England."

His energy and decision.

The enthusiasm which he felt extended itself at once to all around him. He immediately made preparations to put himself at the head of his troops, and march to the eastward, so as to intercept Queen Margaret on her way to London, for he knew that she would, of course, now press forward toward the capital as fast as possible.

He marches to intercept Margaret.

He accordingly set out at once upon his march, and, as he went on, he found that the number of his followers increased very rapidly. The truth was, that the queen's party, by their murder of Richard, and of young Edmund his son, had gone altogether too far for the good of their own cause. The people, when they heard the tidings, were indignant at such cruelty. Those who belonged to the party of the house of York, instead of being intimidated by the severity of the measure, were exasperated at the brutality of it, and they were all eager to join the young duke, Edward, and help him to avenge his father's and his brother's death. Those who had been before on the side of the house of Lancaster were discouraged and repelled, while those who had been doubtful were now ready to declare against the queen.

It is in this way that all excesses in the hour of victory defeat the very ends they were intended to subserve. They weaken the perpetrators, and not the subjects of them.

Warwick.

In the mean time, while young Edward, at the head of his army, was marching on from the westward toward London to intercept the queen, the Earl of Warwick, who has already been mentioned as a friend of Lady Cecily, had also assembled a large force near London, and he was now advancing toward the northward. The poor king was with him. Nominally, the king was in command of the expedition, and every thing was done in his name, but really he was a forlorn and helpless prisoner, forced wholly against his will—so far as the feeble degree of intellect which remained to him enabled him to exercise a will—to seem to head an enterprise directed against his own wife, and his best and strongest friend.

Battle with the queen.
Warwick defeated.
Margaret regains possession of her husband.

The armies of the queen and of the Earl of Warwick advanced toward each other, until they met at last at a short distance north of London. A desperate battle was fought, and the queen's party were completely victorious. When night came on, the Earl of Warwick found that he was beaten at every point, and that his troops had fled in all directions, leaving thousands of the dead and dying all along the road sides. The camp had been abandoned, and there was no time to save any thing; even the poor king was left behind, and the officers of the queen's army found him in a tent, with only one attendant. Of course, the queen was overjoyed at recovering possession of her husband, not merely on his own account personally, but also because she could now act again directly in his name. So she prepared a proclamation, by which the king revoked all that he had done while in the hands of Warwick, on the ground that he had been in durance, and had not acted of his own free will, and also declared Edward a traitor, and offered a large reward for his apprehension.

Excesses committed by the queen's troops.

The queen was now once more filled with exultation and joy. Her joy would have been complete were it not that Edward himself was still to be met, for he was all this time advancing from the westward; she, however, thought that there was not much to be feared from such a boy, Edward being at this time only about nineteen years of age. So the queen moved on toward London, flushed with the victory, and exasperated with the opposition which she had met with. Her soldiers were under very little control, and they committed great excesses. They ravaged the country, and plundered without mercy all those whom they considered as belonging to the opposite party; they committed, too, many atrocious acts of cruelty. It is always thus in civil war. In foreign wars, armies are much more easily kept under control. Troops march through a foreign territory, feeling no personal spite or hatred against the inhabitants of it, for they think it is a matter of course that the people should defend their country and resist invaders. But in a civil war, the men of each party feel a special personal hate against every individual that does not belong to their side, and in periods of actual conflict this hatred becomes a rage that is perfectly uncontrollable.

Accordingly, as the queen and her troops advanced, they robbed and murdered all who came in their way, and they filled the whole country with terror. They even seized and plundered a convent, which was a species of sacrilege. This greatly increased the general alarm. "The wretches!" exclaimed the people, when they heard the tidings, "nothing is sacred in their eyes." The people of London were particularly alarmed. They thought there was danger that the city itself would be given up to plunder if the queen's troops gained admission. So they all turned against her. She sent one day into the town for a supply of provisions, and the authorities, perhaps thinking themselves bound by their official duty to obey orders of this kind coming in the king's name, loaded up some wagons and sent them forth, but the people raised a mob, and stopped the wagons at the gates, refusing to let them go on.

Edward advances.
He enters London.
His welcome.

In the mean time, Edward, growing every hour stronger as he advanced, came rapidly on toward London. He was joined at length by the Earl of Warwick and the remnant of the force which remained to the earl after the battle which he had fought with the queen. The queen, now finding that Edward's strength was becoming formidable, did not dare to meet him; so she retreated toward the north again. Edward, instead of pursuing her, advanced directly toward London. The people threw open the gates to him, and welcomed him as their deliverer. They thronged the streets to look upon him as he passed, and made the air ring with their loud and long acclamations.

Excitement in London.

There was, indeed, every thing in the circumstances of the case to awaken excitement and emotion. Here was a boy not yet out of his teens, extremely handsome in appearance and agreeable in manners, who had taken the field in command of a very large force to avenge the cruel death of his father and brother, and was now coming boldly, at the head of his troops, into the very capital of the king and queen under whose authority his father and brother had been killed.

The most extraordinary circumstance connected with these proceedings was, that during all this time Henry was still acknowledged by every one as the actual king. Edward and his friends maintained, indeed, that he, Edward, was *entitled* to reign, but no one pretended that any thing had yet been done which could have the legal effect of putting him upon the throne. There was, however, now a general expectation that the time for the formal deposition of Henry was near, and in and around London all was excitement and confusion. The people from the surrounding towns flocked every day into the city to see what they could see, and to hear what they could hear. They thronged the streets whenever Edward appeared in public, eager to obtain a glimpse of him.

Measures taken by Edward.

At length, a few days after Edward entered the city, his counselors and friends deemed that the time had come for action. Accordingly, they made arrangements for a grand review in a large open field. Their design was by this review to call together a great concourse of spectators. A vast assembly convened according to their expectations. In the midst of the ceremonies, two noblemen appeared before the multitude to make addresses to them. One of them made a speech in respect to Henry, denouncing the crimes, and the acts of treachery and of oppression which his government had committed. He dilated long on the feebleness and incapacity of the king, and his total inability to exercise any control in the management of public affairs. After he had finished, he called out to the people in a loud voice to declare whether they would submit any longer to have such a man for king.

Voice of the people.

The people answered "NAY, NAY, NAY," with loud and long acclamations.

Then the other speaker made an address in favor of Edward. He explained at length the nature of his title to the crown, showing it to be altogether superior in point of right to that of Henry. He also spoke long and eloquently in praise of Edward's personal qualifications, describing his courage, his activity, and energy, and the various graces and accomplishments for which he was distinguished, in the most glowing terms. He ended by demanding of the people whether they would have Edward for king.

They declare in favor of Edward.

The people answered "YEA, YEA, YEA; KING EDWARD FOREVER! KING EDWARD FOREVER!" with acclamations as long and loud as before.

Of course there could be no legal validity in such proceedings as these, for, even if England had at that time been an elective monarchy, the acclamations of an accidental assembly drawn together to witness a review could on no account have been deemed a valid vote. This ceremony was only meant as a very public announcement of the intention of Edward immediately to assume the throne.

Edward is formally enthroned.
Various ceremonies.

The next day, accordingly, a grand council was held of all the great barons, and nobles, and officers of state. By this council a decree was passed that King Henry, by his late proceedings, had forfeited the crown, and Edward was solemnly declared king in his stead. Immediately afterward, Edward rode at the head of a royal procession, which was arranged for the purpose, to Westminster, and there, in the presence of a vast assembly, he took his seat upon the throne. While there seated, he made a speech to the audience, in which he explained the nature of his hereditary rights, and declared his intention to maintain his rights thenceforth in the most determined manner.

The king now proceeded to Westminster Abbey, where he performed the same ceremonies a second time. He was also publicly proclaimed king on the same day in various parts of London.

Edward marches to the northward.

Edward was now full of ardor and enthusiasm, and his first impulse was to set off, at the head of his army, toward the north, in pursuit of the queen and the old king. The king and queen had gone to York. The queen had not only the king under her care, but also her son, the little Prince of Wales, who was now about eight years old. This young prince was the heir to the crown on the Lancastrian side, and Edward was, of course, very desirous of getting him, as well as the king and queen, into his hands; so he put himself at the head of his troops, and began to move forward as fast as he could go. The body of troops under his command consisted of fifty thousand men. In the queen's army, which was encamped in the neighborhood of York, there were about sixty thousand.

A battle.

Both parties were extremely exasperated against each other, and were eager for the fight. Edward gave orders to his troops to grant no quarter, but, in the event of victory, to massacre without mercy every man that they could bring within their reach. The armies came together at a place called Towton. The combat was begun in the midst of a snow-storm. The armies fought from nine o'clock in the morning till three in the afternoon, and by that time the queen's troops were every where driven from the field. Edward's men pursued them along the roads, slaughtering them without mercy as fast as they could overtake them, until at length nearly forty thousand men were left dead upon the ground.

Edward enters York in triumph.

The queen fled toward the north, taking with her her husband and child. Edward entered York in triumph. At the gates he found the head of his father and that of his brother still remaining upon the poles where the queen had put them. He took them reverently down, and then put other heads in their places, which he cut off for the purpose from some of his prisoners. He was in such a state of fury, that I suppose, if he could have caught the king and queen, he would have cut off *their* heads, and put them on the poles in the place of his father's and his brother's; but he could not catch them. They fled to the north, toward the frontiers of Scotland, and so escaped from his hands.

He inters his father's body.

Edward determined not to pursue the fugitives any farther at that time, as there were many important affairs to be attended to in London, and so he concluded to be satisfied at present with the victory which he had obtained, and with the dispersion of his enemies, and to return to the capital. He first, however, gathered together the remains of his father and brother, and caused them to be buried with solemn funeral ceremonies in one of his castles near York. This was, however, only a temporary arrangement, for, as soon as his affairs were fully settled, the remains were disinterred, and conveyed, with great funeral pomp and parade, to their final resting-place in the southern part of the kingdom.

He returns to London.
Grief of his mother.

As soon as Edward reached London, one of the first things that he did was to send for his two brothers, George and Richard, who, as will be recollected, had been removed by their mother to Holland, and were now in Utrecht pursuing their education. These two boys were all the brothers of Edward that remained now alive. They came back to London. Their widowed mother's heart was filled with a melancholy sort of joy in seeing her children once more together, safe in their native land; but her spirit, after reviving for a moment, sank again, overwhelmed with the bitter and irreparable loss which she had sustained in the death of her husband. His death was, of course, a fatal blow to all those ambitious plans and aspirations which she had cherished for herself. Though the mother of a king, she could now never become herself a queen; and, disappointed and unhappy, she retired to one of the family castles in the neighborhood of London, and lived there comparatively alone and in great seclusion.

Situation of George and Richard.

The boys, on the other hand, were brought forward very conspicuously into public life. In the autumn of the same year in which Edward took possession of the crown, they were made royal dukes, with great parade and ceremony, and were endowed with immense estates to enable them to support the dignity of their rank and position. George was made Duke of Clarence; Richard, Duke of Gloucester; and from this time the two boys were almost always designated by these names.

Suitable persons, too, were appointed to take charge of the boys, for the purpose of conducting their education, and also to manage their estates until they should become of age.

Richard's person.

There have been a great many disputes in respect to Richard's appearance and character at this time. For a long period after his death, people generally believed that he was, from his very childhood, an ugly little monster, that nobody could look upon without fear; and, in fact, he was very repulsive in his personal appearance when he grew up, but at this time of his life the historians and biographers who saw and knew him say that he was quite a pretty boy, though puny and weak. His face was handsome enough, though his form was frail, and not perfectly symmetrical. Those who had charge of him tried to strengthen his constitution by training him to the martial exercises and usages which were practiced in those days, and especially by accustoming him to wear the ponderous armor which was then in use.

Description of the armor worn in those days.

This armor was made of iron or steel. It consisted of a great number of separate pieces, which, when they were all put on, incased almost the whole body, so as to defend it against blows coming from any quarter. First, there was the helmet, or cap of steel, with large oval pieces coming down to protect the ears. Next came the *gorget*, as it was called, which was a sort of collar to cover the neck. Then there were elbow pieces to guard the elbows, and shoulder-plates for the shoulders, and a breast-plate or buckler for the front, and greaves for the legs and thighs. These things were necessary in those days, or at least they were advantageous, for they afforded pretty effectual protection against all the ordinary weapons which were then in use. But they made the warriors themselves so heavy and unwieldy as very greatly to interfere with the freedom of their movements when engaged in battle. There was, indeed, a certain advantage in this weight, as it made the shock with which the knight on horseback encountered his enemy in the charge so much the more heavy and overpowering; but if he were by any accident to lose his seat and fall to the ground, he was generally so encumbered by his armor that he could only partially raise himself therefrom. He was thus compelled to lie almost helpless until his enemy came to kill him, or his squire or some other friend came to help him up.

Necessity of being trained to use this armor.

Of course, to be able to manage one's self at all in these habiliments of iron and steel, there was required not only native strength of constitution, but long and careful training, and it was a very important part of the education of young men of rank in Richard's days to familiarize them with the use of this armor, and inure them to the weight of it. Suits of it were made for boys, the size and weight of each suit being fitted to the form and strength of the wearer. Many of these suits of boys' armor are still preserved in England. There are several specimens to be seen in the Tower of London. They are in the apartment called the Horse Armory, which is a vast hall with effigies of horses, and of men mounted upon them, all completely armed with the veritable suits of steel which the men and the horses that they represent actually wore when they were alive. The horses are arranged along the sides of the room in regular order from the earliest ages down to the time when steel armor of this kind ceased to be worn.

THE OLD QUINTAINE

The armor costly.
Substitutes for it.
Exercises.
Feats to be performed.

These suits of armor were very costly, and the boys for whom they were made were, of course, filled with feelings of exultation and pride when they put them on; and, heavy and uncomfortable as such clothing must have been, they were willing to wear it, and to practice the required exercises in it. When actually made of steel, the armor was very expensive, and such could only be afforded for young princes and nobles of very high rank; for other young men, various substitutes were provided; but all were trained, either in the use of actual armor, or of substitutes, to perform a great number and variety of exercises. They were taught, when they were old enough, to spring upon a horse with as much armor upon them and in their hands as possible; to run races; to see how long they could continue to strike heavy blows in quick succession with a battle-axe or club, as if they were beating an enemy lying upon the ground, and trying to break his armor to pieces; to dance and throw summersets; to mount upon a horse behind another person by leaping from the ground, and assisting themselves only by one hand, and other similar things. One feat which they practiced was to climb up between two partition walls built pretty near together, by bracing their back against one wall, and working with their knees and hands against the other. Another feat was to climb up a ladder on the under side by means of the hands alone.

Account of the quintaine.

Another famous exercise, or perhaps rather game, was performed with what was called the *quintaine*. The quintaine consisted of a stout post set in the ground, and rising about ten or twelve feet above the surface. Across the top was a strong bar, which turned on a pivot made in the top of the post, so that it would go round and round. To one end of this cross-bar there was fixed a square board for a target; to the other end was hung a heavy club. The cross-bar was so poised upon the central pivot that it would move very easily. In playing the game, the competitors, mounted on horseback, were to ride, one after another, under the target-end of the cross-bar, and hurl their spears at it with all their force. The blow from the spear would knock the target-end of the cross-bar away, and so bring round the other end, with its heavy club, to strike a blow on the horseman's head if he did not get instantly out of the way. It was as if he were to strike one enemy in front in battle, while there was another enemy ready on the instant to strike him from behind.

There is one of these ancient quintaines now standing on the green in the village of Offham, in Kent.

Other exercises and sports.
Playing ball.

Such exercises as these were, of course, only fitted for men, or at least for boys who had nearly attained to their full size and strength. There were other games and exercises intended for smaller boys. There are many rude pictures in ancient books illustrating these old games. In one they are playing ball; in another they are playing shuttle-cock. The battle-doors that they use are very rude.

PLAYING BALL

Jumping through a hoop.

These pictures show how ancient these common games are. In another picture the boys are playing with a hoop. Two of them are holding the hoop up between them, and the third is preparing to jump through it, head foremost. His plan is to come down on the other side upon his hands, and so turn a summerset, and come up on his feet beyond.

BATTLE-DOOR AND SHUTTLE-COCK

The two brothers companions.

In these exercises and amusements, and, indeed, in all his occupations, Richard had his brother George, the Duke of Clarence, for his playmate and companion. George was not only older than Richard, but he was also much more healthy and athletic; and some persons have thought that Richard injured himself, and perhaps, in some degree, increased the deformity which he seems to have suffered from in later years, or perhaps brought it on entirely, by overloading himself, in his attempts to keep pace with his brother in these exercises, with burdens of armor, or by straining himself in athletic exertions which were beyond his powers.

Richard's intellectual education.

The intellectual education of the boys was not entirely neglected. They learned to read and write, though they could not write much, or very well. Their names are still found, as they signed them to ancient documents, several of which remain to the present day. The following is a fac-simile of Richard's signature, copied exactly from one of those documents.

RICHARD'S SIGNATURE

Richard continued in this state of pupilage in some of the castles belonging to the family from the time that his brother began to reign until he was about fourteen years of age. Edward, the king, was then twenty-four, and Clarence about seventeen.

Chapter V
Warwick, the King-Maker

A.D. 1461-1468

Situation of Richard under the reign of his brother.

Richard's brother, Edward the Fourth, began to reign when Richard was about eight or nine years of age. His reign continued—with a brief interruption, which will be hereafter explained—for twenty years; so that, for a very important period of his life, after he arrived at some degree of maturity, namely, from the time that he was fourteen to the time that he was thirty, Richard was one of his brother's subjects. He was a prince, it is true, and a prince of the very highest rank—the next person but one, in fact, in the line of succession to the crown. His brother George, the Duke of Clarence, of course, being older than he, came before him; but both the young men, though princes, were subjects. They were under their brother Edward's authority, and bound to serve and obey him as their rightful sovereign; next to him, however, they were the highest personages in the realm. George was, from this time, generally called Clarence, and Richard, Gloucester.

Strange vicissitudes in the life of Margaret.

The reader may perhaps feel some interest and curiosity in learning what became of Queen Margaret and old King Henry after they were driven out of the country toward the north, at the time of Edward's accession. Their prospects seemed, at the time, to be hopelessly ruined, but their case was destined to furnish another very striking instance of the extraordinary reverses of fortune which marked the history of nearly all the great families during the whole course of this York and Lancaster quarrel. In about ten years from the time when Henry and Margaret were driven away, apparently into hopeless exile, they came back in triumph, and were restored to power, and Edward himself, in his turn, was ignominiously expelled from the kingdom. The narrative of the circumstances through which these events were brought about forms quite a romantic story.

In order, however, that this story may be more clearly understood, I will first enumerate the principal personages that take a part in it, and briefly remind the reader of the position which they respectively occupied, and the relations which they sustained to each other.

First, there is the family of King Henry, consisting of himself and his wife, Queen Margaret, and his little son Edward, who had received the title of Prince of Wales. This boy was about eight years old at the time his father and mother were driven away. We left them, in the last chapter, flying toward the frontiers of Scotland to save their lives, leaving to Edward and his troops the full possession of the kingdom.

Henry and his little son, the Prince of Wales, of course represent the house of Lancaster in the dispute for the succession.

Representatives of the house of York.

The house of York was represented by Edward, whose title, as king, was Edward the Fourth, and his two brothers, George and Richard, or, as they were now generally called, Clarence and Gloucester. In case Edward should be married and have a son, his son would succeed him, and George and Richard would be excluded; if, however, he should die without issue, then George would become king; and if George should die without issue, and Richard should survive him, then Richard would succeed. Thus, as matters now stood, George and Richard were presumptive heirs to the crown, and it was natural that they should wish that their brother Edward should never be married.

Margaret.
Value of a marriageable young lady.

Besides these two brothers, who were the only ones of all his brothers that were now living, Edward had a sister named Margaret. Margaret was four years younger than Edward the king, and about six years older than Richard. She was now about seventeen. A young lady of that age in the family of a king in those days was quite a treasure, as the king was enabled to promote his political schemes sometimes very effectually by bestowing her in marriage upon this great prince or that, as would best further the interests which he had in view in foreign courts.

This young lady, Edward's sister, being of the same name—Margaret—with the queen of old King Henry, was distinguished from her by being called Margaret of York, as she belonged to the

York family. The queen was generally known as Margaret of Anjou. Anjou was the place of her nativity.

Warwick.
Warwick becomes Edward's prime minister.

The next great personage to be named is the Earl of Warwick. He was the man, as you will doubtless recollect, who was in command of the sea between England and the Continent at the time when Lady Cecily wished to send her children, George and Richard, away after their father's death, and who assisted in arranging their flight. He was a man of great power and influence, and of such an age and character that he exerted a vast ascendency over all within his influence. Without him, Edward never would have conquered the Lancaster party, and he knew very well that if Warwick, and all those whom Warwick would carry with him, were to desert him, he should not be able to retain his kingdom. Indeed, Warwick received the surname of *King-maker* from the fact that, in repeated instances during this quarrel, he put down one dynasty and raised up the other, just as he pleased. He belonged to a great and powerful family named Neville. As soon as Edward was established on his throne, Warwick, almost as a matter of course, became prime minister. One of his brothers was made chancellor, and a great number of other posts of distinction and honor were distributed among the members of the Neville family. Indeed, although Edward was nominally king, it might have been considered in some degree a question whether it was the house of York or the house of Neville that actually reigned in England.

The Earl of Warwick had two daughters. Their names were Isabella and Anne. These two young ladies the earl reckoned, as Edward did his sister Margaret, among the most important of his political resources. By marrying them to persons of very high position, he could strengthen his alliances and increase his power. There was even a possibility, he thought, of marrying one of them to the King of England, or to a prince who would become king.

The three great parties.

Thus we have for the three great parties to the transactions now to be described, first, the representatives of the house of Lancaster, the feeble Henry, the energetic and strong-minded Margaret of Anjou, and their little son, the Prince of Wales; secondly, the representatives of the house of York, King Edward the Fourth, the two young men his brothers, George, Duke of Clarence, and Richard, Duke of Gloucester, and his sister Margaret; and, thirdly, between these two parties, as it were, the Earl of Warwick and his two daughters, Isabella and Anne, standing at the head of a vast family influence, which ramified to every part of the kingdom, and was powerful enough to give the ascendency to either side, in favor of which they might declare.

The fortunes of Margaret of Anjou.
She escapes to France.

We are now prepared to follow Queen Margaret in her flight toward the north with her husband and her son, at the time when Edward the Fourth overcame her armies and ascended the throne. She pressed on as rapidly as possible, taking the king and the little prince with her, and accompanied and assisted in her flight by a few attendants, till she had crossed the frontier and was safe in Scotland. The Scots espoused her cause, and assisted her to raise fresh troops, with which she made one or two short incursions into England; but she soon found that she could do nothing effectual in this way, and so, after wasting some time in fruitless attempts, she left Scotland with the king and the prince, and went to France.

A new expedition planned.

Here she entered into negotiations with the King of France, and with other princes and potentates, on the Continent, with a view of raising men and money for a new invasion of England. At first these powers declined to assist her. They said that their treasuries were exhausted, and that they had no men. At last, however, Margaret promised to the King of France that if he would furnish her with a fleet and an army, by which she could recover the kingdom of her husband, she would cede to him the town of Calais, which, though situated on the coast of France, was at that time an English possession. This was a very tempting offer, for Calais was a fortress of the first class, and a military post either for England or France of a very important character.

Margaret is defeated and compelled to fly.
She encounters great dangers at sea.

The king consented to this proposal. He equipped a fleet and raised an army, and Margaret set sail for England, taking the king and the prince with her. Her plan was to land in the northern part of the island, near the frontiers of Scotland, where she expected to find the country more friendly to the Lancastrian line than the people were toward the south. As soon as she landed she was joined by many of the people, and she succeeded in capturing some castles and small towns. But the Earl of Warwick, who was, as has been already said, the prime minister under Edward, immediately raised an army of twenty thousand men, and marched to the northward to meet her. Margaret's French army was wholly unprepared to encounter such a force as this, so they fled to their ships. All but about five hundred of the men succeeded in reaching the ships. The five hundred were cut to pieces. Margaret herself was detained in making arrangements for the king and the prince. She concluded not to take them to sea again, but to send them secretly into Wales, while she herself went back to France to see if she could not procure re-enforcements. She barely had time, at last, to reach the ships herself, so close at hand were her enemies. As soon as the queen had embarked, the fleet set sail. The queen had saved nearly all the money and all the stores which she had brought with her from France, and she hoped still to preserve them for another attempt. But the fleet had scarcely got off from the shore when a terrible storm arose, and the ships were all driven upon the rocks and dashed to pieces. The money and the stores were all lost; a large portion of the men were drowned; Margaret herself and the captain of the fleet saved themselves, and, as soon as the storm was over, they succeeded in making their escape back to Berwick in an old fishing-boat which they obtained on the shore.

Soon after this, Margaret, with the captain of the fleet and a very small number of faithful followers who still adhered to her, sailed back again to France.

The king concealed.
The king is made prisoner, and sent to the Tower.

The disturbances, however, which her landing had occasioned, did not cease immediately on her departure. The Lancastrian party all over England were excited and moved to action by the news of her coming, and for two years insurrections were continually taking place, and many battles were fought, and great numbers of people were killed. King Henry was all this time kept in close concealment, sometimes in Wales, and sometimes among the lakes and mountains in Westmoreland. He was conveyed from place to place by his adherents in the most secret manner, the knowledge in respect to his situation being confined to the smallest possible number of persons. This continued for two or three years. At last, however, while the friends of the king were attempting secretly to convey him to a certain castle in Yorkshire, he was seen and recognized by one of his enemies. A plan was immediately formed to make him prisoner. The plan succeeded. The king was surprised by an overwhelming force, which broke into the castle and seized him while he sat at dinner. His captors, and those who were lying in wait to assist them, galloped off at once with their prisoner to London. King Edward shut him up in the Tower, and he remained there, closely confined and strongly guarded for a long time.

Brutal punishments.

Thus King Henry's life was saved, but of those who espoused his cause, and made attempts to restore him, great numbers were seized and beheaded in the most cruel manner. It was Edward's policy to slay all the leaders. It was said that after a battle he would ride with a company of men over the ground, and kill every wounded or exhausted man of rank that still remained alive, though he would spare the common soldiers. Sometimes, when he got men that were specially obnoxious to him into his hands, he would put them to death in the most cruel and ignominious manner. One distinguished knight, that had been taken prisoner by Warwick, was brought to King Edward, who, at that time, as it happened, was sick, and by Edward's orders was treated most brutally. He was first taken out into a public place, and his spurs were struck off from his feet by a cook. This was one of the greatest indignities that a knight could suffer. Then his coat of arms was torn off from him, and another coat, inside out, was put upon him. Then he was made to walk barefoot to the end of the town, and there was laid down upon his back on a sort of drag, and so drawn to the place of execution, where his head was cut off on a block with a broad-axe.

Great exasperation of the combatants.

Such facts as these show what a state of exasperation the two great parties of York and Lancaster were in toward each other throughout the kingdom. It is necessary to understand this, in order fully to appreciate the import and consequences of the very extraordinary transaction which is now to be related.

Account of Elizabeth Woodville.

It seems there was a certain knight named Sir John Gray, a Lancastrian, who had been killed at one of the great battles which had been fought during the war. He had also been attainted, as it was called—that is, sentence had been pronounced against him on a charge of high treason, by which his estates were forfeited, and his wife and children, of course, reduced to poverty. The name of his wife was Elizabeth Woodville. She was the daughter of a noble knight named Sir Richard Woodville. Her mother's name was Jacquetta. On the death and attainder of her husband, being reduced to great poverty and distress, she went home to the house of her father and mother, at a beautiful manor which they possessed at Grafton. She was quite young, and very beautiful.

Edward's first interview with her.
The secret marriage.

It happened that by some means or other Edward paid a visit one day to the Lady Jacquetta, at her manor, as he was passing through the country. Whether this visit was accidental, or whether it was contrived by Jacquetta, does not appear. However this may be, the beautiful widow came into the presence of the king, and, throwing herself at his feet, begged and implored him to revoke the attainder of her husband for the sake of her innocent and helpless children. The king was much moved by her beauty and by her distress. From pitying her he soon began to love her. And yet it seemed impossible that he should marry her. Her rank, in the first place, was far below his, and then, what was worse, she belonged to the Lancastrian party, the king's implacable enemies. The king knew very well that all his own partisans would be made furious at the idea of such a match, and that, if they knew that it was in contemplation, they would resist it to the utmost of their power. For a time he did not know what he should do. At length, however, his love for the beautiful widow, as might easily be foreseen, triumphed over all considerations of prudence, and he was secretly married to her. The marriage took place in the morning, in a very private manner, in the month of May, in 1464.

The marriage gradually revealed.

The king kept the marriage secret nearly all summer. He thought it best to break the subject to his lords and nobles gradually, as he had opportunity to communicate it to them one by one. In this way it at length became known, without producing, at any one time, any special sensation, and toward the fall preparations were made for openly acknowledging the union.

Ancient portrait of Edward IV

KING EDWARD IV

This engraving is a portrait of King Edward as he appeared at this time. It is copied from an ancient painting, and doubtless represents correctly the character and expression of his countenance, and one form, at least, of dress which he was accustomed to wear. He was, at the time of his marriage, about twenty-two years of age. Elizabeth was ten years older.

Portrait of Queen Elizabeth Woodville.

QUEEN ELIZABETH WOODVILLE
46

This engraving represents the queen. It is taken, like the other, from an ancient portrait, and no doubt corresponds closely to the original.

Indignation of the Earl of Warwick.

Although the knowledge of the king's marriage produced no sudden outbreak of opposition, it awakened a great deal of secret indignation and rage, and gave occasion to many suppressed mutterings and curses. Of course, every leading family of the realm, that had been on Edward's side in the civil wars, which contained a marriageable daughter, had been forming hopes and laying plans to secure this magnificent match for themselves. Those who had no marriageable daughters of their own joined their nearest relatives and friends in their schemes, or formed plans for some foreign alliance with a princess of France, or Burgundy, or Holland, whichever would best harmonize with the political schemes that they wished to promote. The Earl of Warwick seems to have belonged to the former class. He had two daughters, as has already been stated. It would very naturally be his desire that the king, if he were to take for his wife any English subject at all, should make choice of one of these. Of course, he was more than all the rest irritated and vexed at what the king had done. He communicated his feelings to Clarence, but concealed them from the king. Clarence was, of course, ready to sympathize with the earl. He was ready enough to take offense at any thing connected with the king's marriage on very slight grounds, for it was very much for his interest, as the next heir, that his brother should not be married at all.

WESTMINSTER IN TIMES OF PUBLIC CELEBRATIONS

George and Richard.
The queen is publicly acknowledged.

The earl and Clarence, however, thought it best for the time to suppress and conceal their opposition to the marriage; so they joined very readily in the ceremonies connected with the public acknowledgment of the queen. A vast assemblage of nobles, prelates, and other grand dignitaries was convened, and Elizabeth was brought forward before them and formally presented. The Earl of Warwick and Clarence appeared in the foremost rank among her friends on this occasion. They took her by the hand, and, leading her forward, presented her to the assembled multitude of lords and ladies, who welcomed her with long and loud acclamations.

Soon after this a grand council was convened, and a handsome income was settled upon the queen, to enable her properly to maintain the dignity of her station.

Early in the next year preparations were made for a grand coronation of the queen. Foreign princes were invited to attend the ceremony, and many came, accompanied by large bodies of knights and squires, to do honor to the occasion. The coronation took place in May. The queen was conveyed in procession through the streets of London on a sort of open palanquin, borne by horses most magnificently caparisoned. Vast crowds of people assembled along the streets to look at the procession as it passed. The next day the coronation itself took place in Westminster, and it was followed by games, feasts, tournaments, and public rejoicings of every kind, which lasted many days.

Various difficulties and entanglements resulting from this marriage.

Thus far every thing on the surface, at least, had gone well; but it was not long after the coronation before the troubles which were to be expected from such a match began to develop themselves in great force. The new queen was ambitious, and she was naturally desirous of bringing her friends forward into places of influence and honor. The king was, of course, ready to listen to her recommendations; but then all her friends were Lancastrians. They were willing enough, it is true, to change their politics and to become Yorkists for the sake of the rewards and honors which they could obtain by the change, but the old friends of the king were greatly exasperated to find the important posts, one after another, taken away from them, and given to their hated enemies.

Jealousy against the queen's family and relations.

Then, besides the quarrel for the political offices, there were a great many of the cherished matrimonial plans and schemes of the old families interfered with and broken up by the queen's family thus coming into power. It happened that the queen had five unmarried sisters. She began to form plans for securing for them men of the highest rank and position in the realm. This, of course, thwarted the plans and disappointed the hopes of all those families who had been scheming to gain these husbands for their own daughters. To see five great heirs of dukes and barons thus withdrawn from the matrimonial market, and employed to increase the power and prestige of their ancient and implacable foes, filled the souls of the old Yorkist families with indignation. Parties were formed. The queen and her family and friends—the Woodvilles and Grays—with all their adherents, were on one side; the Neville family, with the Earl of Warwick at their head, and most of the old Yorkist noblemen, were on the other; Clarence joined the Earl of Warwick; Richard, on the other hand, or Gloucester, as he was now called, adhered to the king.

Situation of Henry and his family.

Things went on pretty much in this way for two years. There was no open quarrel, though there was a vast deal of secret animosity and bickering. The great world at court was divided into two sets, or cliques, that hated each other very cordially, though both, for the present, pretended to support King Edward as the rightful sovereign of the country. The struggle was for the honors and offices under him. The families who still adhered to the old Lancastrian party, and to the rights of Henry and of the little Prince of Wales, withdrew, of course, altogether from the court, and, retiring to their castles, brooded moodily there over their fallen fortunes, and waited in expectation of better times. Henry was imprisoned in the Tower; Margaret and the Prince of Wales were on the Continent. They and their friends were, of course, watching the progress of the quarrel between the party of the Earl of Warwick and that of the king, hoping that it might at last lead to an open rupture, in which case the Lancastrians might hope for Warwick's aid to bring them again into power.

Margaret of York.

And now another circumstance occurred which widened this breach very much indeed. It arose from a difference of opinion between King Edward and the Earl of Warwick in respect to the marriage of the king's sister Margaret, known, as has already been said, as Margaret of York. There was upon the Continent a certain Count Charles, the son and heir of the Duke of Burgundy, who demanded her hand. The count's family had been enemies of the house of York, and had done every thing in their power to promote Queen Margaret's plans, so long as there was any hope for her; but when they found that King Edward was firmly established on the throne, they came over to his side, and now the count demanded the hand of the Princess Margaret in marriage; but the stern old Earl of Warwick did not like such friendship as this, so he recommended that the count should be refused, and that Margaret should have for her husband one of the princes of France.

WARWICK IN THE PRESENCE OF THE FRENCH KING

Plans and manoeuvres in respect to Margaret's marriage.

Now King Edward himself preferred Count Charles for the husband of Margaret, and this chiefly because the queen, his wife, preferred him on account of the old friendship which had subsisted between his family and the Lancastrians. Besides this, however, Flanders, the country over which the count was to reign on the death of his father, was at that time so situated that an alliance with it would be of

50

greater advantage to Edward's political plans than an alliance with France. But, notwithstanding this, the earl was so earnest in urging his opinion, that finally Edward yielded, and the earl was dispatched to France to negotiate the marriage with the French prince.

The earl set off on this embassy in great magnificence. He landed in Normandy with a vast train of attendants, and proceeded in almost royal state toward Paris. The King of France, to honor his coming and the occasion, came forth to meet him. The meeting took place at Rouen. The proposals were well received by the French king. The negotiations were continued for eight or ten days, and at last every thing was arranged. For the final closing of the contract, it was necessary that a messenger from the King of France should proceed to London. The king appointed an archbishop and some other dignitaries to perform the service. The earl then returned to England, and was soon followed by the French embassadors, expecting that every thing essential was settled, and that nothing but a few formalities remained.

Count Charles carries the day.

But, in the mean time, while all this had been going on in France, Count Charles had quietly sent an embassador to England to press his claim to the princess's hand. This messenger managed this business very skillfully, so as not to attract any public attention to what he was doing; and besides, the earl being away, the queen, Elizabeth, could exert all her influence over her husband's mind unimpeded. Edward was finally persuaded to promise Margaret's hand to the count, and the contracts were made; so that, when the earl and the French embassadors arrived, they found, to their astonishment and dismay, that a rival and enemy had stepped in during their absence and secured the prize.

Vexation of Warwick.

The Earl of Warwick was furious when he learned how he had been deceived. He had been insulted, he said, and disgraced. Edward made no attempt to pacify him; indeed, any attempt that he could have made would probably have been fruitless. The earl withdrew from the court, went off to one of his castles, and shut himself up there in great displeasure.

Progress of the quarrel.

The quarrel now began to assume a very serious air. Edward suspected that the earl was forming plots and conspiracies against him. He feared that he was secretly designing to take measures for restoring the Lancastrian line to the throne. He was alarmed for his personal safety. He expelled all Warwick's family and friends from the court, and, whenever he went out in public, he took care to be always attended by a strong body-guard, as if he thought there was danger of an attempt upon his life.

A temporary reconciliation.

At length one of the earl's brothers, the youngest of the family, who was at that time Archbishop of York, interposed to effect a reconciliation. We have not space here to give a full account of the negotiations; but the result was, a sort of temporary peace was made, by which the earl again returned to court, and was restored apparently to his former position. But there was no cordial good-will between him and the king. Edward dreaded the earl's power, and hated the stern severity of his character, while the earl, by the commanding influence which he exerted in the realm, was continually thwarting both Edward and Elizabeth in their plans.

A new marriage scheme.
Edward displeased.

Edward and Elizabeth had now been married some time, but they had no son, and, of course, no heir, for daughters in those days did not inherit the English crown. Of course, Clarence, Edward's second brother, was the next heir. This increased the jealousy which the two brothers felt toward each other, and tended very much to drive Clarence away from Edward, and to increase the intimacy between Clarence and Warwick. At length, in 1468, it was announced that a marriage was in contemplation between Clarence and Isabella, the Earl of Warwick's oldest daughter. Edward and Queen Elizabeth were very much displeased and very much alarmed when they heard of this plan. If carried into effect, it would bind Clarence and the Warwick influence together in indissoluble bonds, and make their power much more formidable than ever before. Every body would say when the marriage was concluded,

"Now, in case Edward should die, which event may happen at any time, the earl's daughter will be queen, and then the earl will have a greater influence than ever in the disposition of offices and honors.

It behooves us, therefore, to make friends with him in season, so as to secure his good-will in advance, before he comes into power."

He fails of preventing the marriage.
The ceremony performed at Calais.

King Edward and his queen, seeing how much this match was likely at once to increase the earl's importance, did every thing in their power to prevent it. But they could not succeed. The earl was determined that Clarence and his daughter should be married. The opposition was, however, so strong at court that the marriage could not be celebrated at London; so the ceremony was performed at Calais, which city was at that time under the earl's special command. The king and queen remained at London, and made no attempt to conceal their vexation and chagrin.

Chapter VI
The Downfall of York

1469-1470

Insurrections.
The king goes to meet the rebels.

Edward's apprehension and anxiety in respect to the danger that Warwick might be concocting schemes to restore the Lancastrian line to the throne were greatly increased by the sudden breaking out of insurrections in the northern part of the island, while Warwick and Clarence were absent in Calais, on the occasion of Clarence's marriage to Isabella. The insurgents did not demand the restoration of the Lancastrian line, but only the removal of the queen's family and relations from the council. The king raised an armed force, and marched to the northward to meet the rebels. But his army was disaffected, and he could do nothing. They fled before the advancing army of insurgents, and Edward went with them to Nottingham Castle, where he shut himself up, and wrote urgently to Warwick and Clarence to come to his aid.

Rebellion suppressed.

Warwick made no haste to obey this command. After some delay, however, he left Calais in command of one of his lieutenants and repaired to Nottingham, where he soon released the king from his dangerous situation. He quelled the rebellion too, but not until the insurgents had seized the father and one of the brothers of the queen, and cut off their heads.

In the mean time, the Lancastrians themselves, thinking that this was a favorable time for them, began to put themselves in motion. Warwick was the only person who was capable of meeting them and putting them down. This he did, taking the king with him in his train, in a condition more like that of a prisoner than a sovereign. At length, however, the rebellions were suppressed, and all parties returned to London.

A grand reconciliation.

There now took place what purported to be a grand reconciliation. Treaties were drawn up and signed between Warwick and Clarence on one side, and the king on the other, by which both parties bound themselves to forgive and forget all that had passed, and thenceforth to be good friends; but, notwithstanding all the solemn signings and sealings with which these covenants were secured, the actual condition of the parties in respect to each other remained entirely unchanged, and neither of the three felt a whit more confidence in the others after the execution of these treaties than before.

At last the secret distrust which they felt toward each other broke out openly. Warwick's brother, the Archbishop of York, made an entertainment at one of his manors for a party of guests, in which were included the king, the Duke of Clarence, and the Earl of Warwick. It was about three months after the treaties were signed that this entertainment was made, and the feast was intended to celebrate and cement the good understanding which it was now agreed was henceforth to prevail. The king arrived at the manor, and, while he was in his room making his toilet for the supper, which was all ready to be served, an attendant came to him and whispered in his ear,

"Your majesty is in danger. There is a band of armed men in ambush near the house."

The king frightened.

The king was greatly alarmed at hearing this. He immediately stole out of the house, mounted his horse, and, with two or three followers, rode away as fast as he could ride. He continued his journey all night, and in the morning arrived at Windsor Castle.

The quarrel renewed.
New reconciliations.

Then followed new negotiations between Warwick and the king, with mutual reproaches, criminations, and recriminations without number. Edward insisted that treachery was intended at the house to which he had been invited, and that he had barely escaped, by his sudden flight, from falling into the snare. But Warwick and his friends denied this entirely, and attributed the flight of the king to a wholly unreasonable alarm, caused by his jealous and suspicious temper. At last Edward suffered himself to be reassured, and then came new treaties and a new reconciliation.

New rebellions.

This peace was made in the fall of 1469, and in the spring of 1470 a new insurrection broke out. The king believed that Warwick himself, and Clarence, were really at the bottom of these disturbances, but still he was forced to send them with bodies of troops to subdue the rebels; he, however, immediately raised a large army for himself, and proceeded to the seat of war. He reached the spot before Warwick and Clarence arrived there. He gave battle to the insurgents, and defeated them. He took a great many prisoners, and beheaded them. He found, or pretended to find, proof that Warwick and Clarence, instead of intending to fight the insurgents, had made their arrangements for joining them on the following day, and that he had been just in time to defeat their treachery. Whether he really found evidence of these intentions on the part of Warwick and Clarence or not, or whether he was flushed by the excitement of victory, and resolved to seize the occasion to cut loose at once and forever from the entanglement in which he had been bound, is somewhat uncertain. At all events, he now declared open war against Warwick and Clarence, and set off immediately on his march to meet them, at the head of a force much superior to theirs.

Warwick comes to open war with the king.

Warwick and Clarence marched and countermarched, and made many manoeuvres to escape a battle, and during all this time their strength was rapidly diminishing. As long as they were nominally on the king's side, however really hostile to him, they had plenty of followers; but, now that they were in open war against him, their forces began to melt away. In this emergency, Warwick suddenly changed all his plans. He disbanded his army, and then taking all his family with him, including Clarence and Isabella, and accompanied by an inconsiderable number of faithful friends, he marched at the head of a small force which he retained as an escort to the sea-port of Dartmouth, and then embarked for Calais.

The vessels employed to transport the party formed quite a little fleet, so numerous were the servants and attendants that accompanied the fugitives. They embarked without delay on reaching the coast, as they were in haste to make the passage and arrive at Calais, for Isabella, Clarence's wife, was about to become a mother, and at Calais they thought that they should all be, as it were, at home.

It will be remembered that the Earl of Warwick was the governor of Calais, and that when he left it he had appointed a lieutenant to take command of it during his absence. Before his ship arrived off the port this lieutenant had received dispatches from Edward, which had been hurried to him by a special messenger, informing him that Warwick was in rebellion against his sovereign, and forbidding the lieutenant to allow him or his party to enter the town.

Warwick and his party not allowed to land at Calais.

Accordingly, when Warwick's fleet arrived off the port, they found the guns of the batteries pointed at them, and sentinels on the piers warning them not to attempt to land.

The party in great straits.

Warwick was thunderstruck. To be thus refused admission to his own fortress by his own lieutenant was something amazing, as well as outrageous. The earl was at first completely bewildered; but, on demanding an explanation, the lieutenant sent him word that the refusal to land was owing to the people of the town. They, he said, having learned that he and the king had come to open war, insisted that the fortress should be reserved for their sovereign. Warwick then explained the situation that his daughter was in; but the lieutenant was firm. The determination of the people was so strong, he said, that he could not control it. Finally, the child was born on board the ship, as it lay at anchor off the port, and all the aid or comfort which the party could get from the shore consisted of two flagons of wine, which the lieutenant, with great hesitation and reluctance, allowed to be sent on board. The child was a son. His birth was an event of great importance, for he was, of course, as Clarence's son, a prince in the direct line of succession to the English crown.

They land at Harfleur.

At length, finding that he could not land at Calais, Warwick sailed away with his fleet along the coast of France till he reached the French port of Harfleur. Here his ships were admitted, and the whole party were allowed to land.

Strange compact between Warwick and Queen Margaret.

Then followed various intrigues, manoeuvres, and arrangements, which we have not time here fully to unravel; but the end of all was, that in a few weeks after the Earl of Warwick's landing in France, he repaired to a castle where Margaret of Anjou and her son, the Prince of Wales, were residing, and there, in the course of a short time, he made arrangements to espouse her cause, and assist in restoring her husband to the English throne, on condition that her son, the Prince of Wales, should marry his second daughter Anne. It is said that Queen Margaret for a long time refused to consent to this arrangement. She was extremely unwilling that her son, the heir to the English crown, should take for a wife the daughter of the hated enemy to whom the downfall of her family, and all the terrible calamities which had befallen them, had been mainly owing. She was, however, at length induced to yield. Her ambition gained the victory over her hate, and she consented to the alliance on a solemn oath being taken by Warwick that thenceforth he would be on her side, and do all in his power to restore her family to the throne.

This arrangement was accordingly carried into effect, and thus the earl had one of his daughters married to the next heir to the English crown in the line of York, and the other to the next heir in the line of Lancaster. He had now only to choose to which dynasty he would secure the throne. Of course, the oath which he had taken, like other political oaths taken in those days, was only to be kept so long as he should deem it for his interest to keep it.

Attempt to entice Clarence away from Warwick.

He could not at once openly declare in favor of King Henry, for fear of alienating Clarence from him. But Clarence was soon drawn away. King Edward, when he heard of the marriage of Warwick's daughter with the Prince of Wales, immediately formed a plan for sending a messenger to negotiate with Clarence. He could not do this openly, for he knew very well that Warwick would not allow any avowed messenger from Edward to land; so he sent a lady. The lady was a particular friend of Isabella, Clarence's wife. She traveled privately by the way of Calais. On the way she said nothing about the object of her journey, but gave out simply that she was going to join her mistress, the Princess Isabella. On her arrival she managed the affair with great discretion. She easily obtained private interviews with Clarence, and represented to him that Warwick, now that his daughter was married to the heir on the Lancastrian side, would undoubtedly lay all his plans forthwith for putting that family on the throne, and that thus Clarence would lose all.

"And therefore," said she, "how much better it will be for you to leave him and return to your brother Edward, who is ready to forgive and forget all the past, and receive you again as his friend."

Clarence was convinced by these representations, and soon afterward, watching his opportunity, he made his way to England, and there espoused his brother's cause, and was received again into his service.

Edward does not fear.

In the mean time, tidings were continually coming to King Edward from his friends on the Continent, warning him of Warwick's plans, and bidding him to be upon his guard. But Edward had no fear. He said he wished that Warwick would come.

"All I ask of my friends on the other side of the Channel," said he, "is that, when he does come, they will not let him get away again before I catch him—as he did before."

The Duke of Burgundy.

Edward's great friend across the Channel was his brother-in-law, the Duke of Burgundy, the same who, when Count Charles, had married the Princess Margaret of York, as related in a former chapter. The Duke of Burgundy prepared and equipped a fleet, and had it all in readiness to intercept the earl in case he should attempt to sail for England.

Queen Margaret crosses the Channel.

In the mean time, Queen Margaret and the earl went on with their preparations. The King of France furnished them with men, arms, and money. When every thing was ready, the earl sent word to the north of England, to some of his friends and partisans there, to make a sort of false insurrection, in order to entice away Edward and his army from the capital. This plan succeeded. Edward heard of the rising, and, collecting all the troops which were at hand, he marched to the northward to put it down. Just at this time a sudden storm arose and dispersed the Duke of Burgundy's fleet. The earl then immediately put to sea, taking with him Margaret of Anjou and her son, the Prince of Wales, with his wife, the Earl of Warwick's daughter. The Prince of Wales was now about eighteen years old. The father, King Henry, Margaret's husband, was not joined with the party. He was all this time, as you will recollect, a prisoner in the

Tower, where Warwick himself had shut him up when he deposed him in order to place Edward upon the throne.

All Europe looked on with astonishment at these proceedings, and watched the result with intense interest. Here was a man who, having, by a desperate and bloody war, deposed a king, and shut him up in prison, and compelled his queen and the prince his son, the heir, to fly from the country to save their lives, had now sought the exiles in their banishment, had married his own daughter to the prince, and was setting forth on an expedition for the purpose of liberating the father again, and restoring him to the throne.

Landing of the expedition.
Reception of it.

The earl's fleet crossed the Channel safely, and landed on the coast of Devonshire, in the southwestern part of the island. The landing of the expedition was the signal for great numbers of the nobles and high families throughout the realm to prepare for changing sides; for it was the fact, throughout the whole course of these wars between the houses of York and Lancaster, that a large proportion of the nobility and gentry, and great numbers of other adventurers, who lived in various ways on the public, stood always ready at once to change sides whenever there was a prospect that another side was coming into power. Then there were, in such a case as this, great numbers who were secretly in favor of the Lancaster line, but who were prevented from manifesting their preference while the house of York was in full possession of power. All these persons were aroused and excited by the landing of Warwick. King Edward found that his calls upon his friends to rally to his standard were not promptly obeyed. His friends were beginning to feel some doubt whether it would be best to continue his friends. A certain preacher in London had the courage to pray in public for the "king in the Tower," and the manner in which this allusion was received by the populace, and the excitement which it produced, showed how ready the city of London was to espouse Henry's cause.

Edward's friends and followers forsake him.

These, and other such indications, alarmed Edward very much. He turned to the southward again when he learned that Warwick had landed. Richard, who had, during all this period, adhered faithfully to Edward's cause, was with him, in command of a division of the army. As Warwick himself was rapidly advancing toward the north at this time, the two armies soon began to approach each other. As the time of trial drew nigh, Edward found that his friends and supporters were rapidly abandoning him. At length, one day, while he was at dinner, a messenger came in and told him that one of the leading officers of the army, with the whole division under his command, were waving their caps and cheering for "King Harry." He saw at once that all was lost, and he immediately prepared to fly.

Edward flies from the country.

He was not far from the eastern coast at this time, and there was a small vessel there under his orders, which had been employed in bringing provisions from the Thames to supply his army. There were also two Dutch vessels there. The king took possession of these vessels, with Richard, and the few other followers that went with him, and put at once to sea. Nobody knew where they were going.

Difficulties and dangers.

Very soon after they had put to sea they were attacked by pirates. They escaped only by running their vessel on shore on the coast of Finland. Here the king found himself in a state of almost absolute destitution, so that he had to pawn his clothing to satisfy the most urgent demands. At length, after meeting with various strange adventures, he found his way to the Hague, where he was, for the time, in comparative safety.

As soon as Warwick ascertained that Edward had fled, he turned toward London, with nothing now to impede his progress. He entered London in triumph. Clarence joined him, and entered London in his train; for Clarence, though he had gone to England with the intention of making common cause with his brother, had not been able yet to decide positively whether it would, on the whole, be for his interest to do so, and had, accordingly, kept himself in some degree uncommitted, and now he turned at once again to Warwick's side.

The queen—Elizabeth Woodville—with her mother Jacquetta, were residing at the Tower at this time, where they had King Henry in their keeping; for the Tower was an extended group of buildings, in which palace and prison were combined in one. As soon as the queen learned that Edward was defeated, and that Warwick and Clarence were coming in triumph to London, she took her mother and three of her daughters—Elizabeth, Mary, and Cecily—who were with her at that time, and also a lady attendant, and hurried down the Tower stairs to a barge which was always in waiting there. She embarked on board the barge, and ordered the men to row her up to Westminster.

His mother makes her escape to sanctuary.

Westminster is at the upper end of London, as the Tower is at the lower. On arriving at Westminster, the whole party fled for refuge to a sanctuary there. This sanctuary was a portion of the sacred precincts of a church, from which a refugee could not be taken, according to the ideas of those times, without committing the dreadful crime of sacrilege. A part of the building remained standing for three hundred years after this time, as represented in the opposite engraving. It was a gloomy old edifice, and it must have been a cheerless residence for princesses and a queen.

THE SANCTUARY

Birth of Edward's son and heir.

In this sanctuary, the queen, away from her husband, and deprived of almost every comfort, gave birth to her first son. Some persons living near took compassion upon her forlorn and desolate condition, and rendered her such aid as was absolutely necessary, out of charity. The abbot of the monastery connected with the church sent in various conveniences, and a good woman named Mother Cobb, who lived near by, came in and acted as nurse for the mother and the child.

The child was baptized in the sanctuary a few days after he was born. He was named Edward, after his father. Of course, the birth of this son of King Edward cut off Clarence and his son from the succession on the York side. This little Edward was now the heir, and, about thirteen years after this, as we shall see in the sequel, he became King of England.

King Henry is fully restored to the throne.

As soon as the Earl of Warwick reached London, he proceeded at once to the Tower to release old King Henry from his confinement. He found the poor king in a wretched plight. His apartment was gloomy and comfortless, his clothing was ragged, and his person squalid and dirty. The earl brought him forth from his prison, and, after causing his personal wants to be properly attended to, clothed him once more in royal robes, and conveyed him in state through London to the palace in Westminster, and established him there nominally as King of England, though Warwick was to all intents and purposes the real king. A Parliament was called, and all necessary laws were passed to sanction and confirm the dynasty. Queen Margaret, who, however, had not yet arrived from the Continent, was restored to her former rank, and the young Prince of Wales, now about eighteen years old, was the object of universal interest throughout the kingdom, as now the unquestioned and only heir to the crown.

Position of Richard.

It was in the month of October, 1470, that old King Henry and his family were restored to the throne. Clarence, as we have seen, being allied to Warwick by being married to his daughter, was induced to go over with him to the Lancastrian side; but Gloucester—that is, Richard—remained true to his own line, and followed the fortunes of his brother, in adverse as well as in prosperous times, with unchanging fidelity. He was now with Edward in the dominions of the Duke of Burgundy, who, you will recollect, married Margaret, Edward's sister, and who was now very naturally inclined to espouse Edward's cause.

The Duke of Burgundy.
His cunning.

The Duke of Burgundy did not, however, dare to espouse Edward's cause too openly, for fear of the King of France, who took the side of Henry and Queen Margaret. He, however, did all in his power secretly to befriend him. Edward and Richard began immediately to form schemes for going back to England and recovering possession of the kingdom. The Duke of Burgundy issued a public proclamation, in which it was forbidden that any of his subjects should join Edward, or that any expedition to promote his designs should be fitted out in any part of his dominions. This proclamation was for the sake of the King of France. At the same time that he issued these orders publicly, he secretly sent Edward a large sum of money, furnished him with a fleet of fifteen or twenty ships, and assisted him in collecting a force of twelve hundred men.

Secret communication with Clarence.
Warwick's plans to secure Clarence.

While he was making these arrangements and preparations on the Continent, Edward and his friends had also opened a secret communication with Clarence in England. It would, of course, very much weaken the cause of Edward and Richard to have Clarence against them; so Margaret, the wife of the Duke of Burgundy, interested herself in endeavoring to win him back again to their side. She had herself great influence over him, and she was assisted in her efforts by their mother, the Lady Cecily, who was still living in the neighborhood of London, and who was greatly grieved at Clarence's having turned against his brothers. The tie which bound Clarence to the Earl of Warwick was, of course, derived chiefly from his being married to Warwick's daughter. Warwick, however, did not trust wholly to this. As soon as he had restored Henry to the throne, he contrived a cunning plan which he thought would tend to bind Clarence still more strongly to himself, and to alienate him completely from Edward. This plan was to induce the Parliament to confiscate all Edward's estates and confer them upon Clarence.

"Now," said Warwick to himself, when this measure had been accomplished, "Clarence will be sure to oppose Edward's return to England, for he knows very well that if he should return and be restored to the throne, he would, of course, take all these estates back again."

But, while Edward was forming his plans on the Continent for a fresh invasion of England, Margaret sent messengers to Clarence, and their persuasions, united to those of his mother, induced Clarence to change his mind. He was governed by no principle whatever in what he did, but only looked to see what would most speedily and most fully gratify his ambition and increase his wealth. So, when they argued that it would be much better for him to be on the side of his brothers, and assist in restoring his own branch of the family to the throne, than to continue his unnatural connection with Warwick and the house of Lancaster, he allowed himself to be easily persuaded, and he promised that though, for the present, he should remain ostensibly a friend of Warwick, still, if Edward and Richard would raise an expedition and come to England, he would forsake Warwick and the Lancasters, and join them.

Edward and Richard sail for England.

Accordingly, in the spring, when the fleet and the forces were ready, Edward and Richard set sail from the Low Country to cross the Channel. It was early in March. They intended to proceed to the north of England and land there. They had a very stormy passage, and in the end the fleet was dispersed, and Edward and Richard with great difficulty succeeded in reaching the land. The two brothers were in different ships, and they landed in different places, a few miles apart from each other. Their situation was now extremely critical, for all England was in the power of Warwick and the Lancastrians, and Edward and Richard were almost entirely without men.

They, however, after a time, got together a small force, consisting chiefly of the troops who had come with them, and who had succeeded at last in making their way to the land. At the head of this force they advanced into the country toward the city of York. Edward gave out every where that he had not come with any view of attempting to regain possession of the throne, but only to recover his own private and family estates, which had been unjustly confiscated, he said, and conferred upon his brother. He acquiesced entirely, he said, in the restoration of Henry to the throne, and acknowledged him as king, and solemnly declared that he would not do any thing to disturb the peace of the country.

Stratagems of war.

All this was treacherous and false; but Edward and Richard thought that they were not yet strong enough to announce openly their real designs, and, in the mean time, the uttering of any false declarations which they might deem it good policy to make was to be considered as a stratagem justified by usage, as one of the legitimate resources of war.

Reception of Edward at York.

So they went on, nobody opposing them. They reached, at length, the city of York. Here Edward met the mayor and aldermen of the city, and renewed his declaration, which he confirmed by a solemn oath, that he never would lay any claim to the throne of England, or do any thing to disturb King Henry in his possession of it. He cried out, in a loud voice, in the hearing of the people, "Long live King Henry, and Prince Edward his son!" He wore an ostrich feather, too, in his armor, which was the badge of Prince Edward. The people of York were satisfied with these protestations, and allowed him to proceed.

The roses.
Public opinion.

His force was continually increasing as he advanced, and at length, on crossing the River Trent, he came to a part of the country where almost the whole population had been on the side of York during all the previous wars. He began now to throw off his disguise, and to avow more openly that his object was again to obtain possession of the throne for the house of York. His troops now began to exhibit the white rose, which for many generations had been the badge of the house of York, as the red rose had been that of Lancaster. [4] In a word, the country was every where aroused and excited by the idea that another revolution was impending, and all those whose ruling principle it was to be always with the party that was uppermost began to make preparations for coming over to Edward's side.

Warwick.
Position of Clarence.
His double dealing.

In the mean time, however, Warwick, alarmed, had come from the northward to London to meet the invaders at the head of a strong force. Clarence was in command of one great division of this force, and Warwick himself of the other. The two bodies of troops marched at some little distance from each other. Edward shaped his course so as to approach that commanded by Clarence. Warwick did all he could to prevent this, being, apparently, somewhat suspicious that Clarence was not fully to be relied on. But Edward succeeded, by dint of skillful manoeuvring, in accomplishing his object, and thus he and Clarence came into the neighborhood of each other. The respective encampments were only three miles apart. It seems, however, that there were still some closing negotiations to be made before Clarence was fully prepared to take the momentous step that was now before him. Richard was the agent of these negotiations. He went back and forth between the two camps, conveying the proposals and counter-proposals from one party to the other, and doing all in his power to remove obstacles from the way, and to bring his brothers to an agreement. At last every thing was arranged. Clarence ordered his men to display the white rose upon their armor, and then, with trumpets sounding and banners flying, he marched forth to meet Edward, and to submit himself to his command.

Clarence goes over to Edward's side.

When the column which he led arrived near to Edward's camp, it halted, and Clarence himself, with a small body of attendants,

---

advanced to meet his brother; Edward, at the same time, leaving his encampment, in company with Richard and several noblemen, came forward too. Thus Edward and Clarence met, as the old chronicle expresses it, "betwixt both hosts, where was right kind and loving language betwixt them two. And then, in like wise, spoke together the two Dukes of Clarence and Gloucester, and afterward the other noblemen that were there with them; whereof all the people that were there that loved them were right glad and joyous, and thanked God highly for that joyous meeting, unity and concord, hoping that thereby should grow unto them prosperous fortune in all that they should after that have to do."

Warwick was, of course, in a dreadful rage when he learned that Clarence had betrayed him and gone over to the enemy. He could do nothing, however, to repair the mischief, and he was altogether too weak to resist the two armies now combined against him; so he drew back, leaving the way clear, and Edward, at the head now of an overwhelming force, and accompanied by both his brothers, advanced directly to London.

Edward triumphant.

He was received at the capital with great favor. Whoever was uppermost for the time being was always received with favor in England in those days, both in the capital and throughout the country at large. It was said, however, that the interest in Edward's fortunes, and in the succession of his branch of the family to the throne, was greatly increased at this time by the birth of his son, which had taken place in the sanctuary, as related in the last chapter, soon after Queen Elizabeth sought refuge there, at the time of Edward's expulsion from the kingdom. Of course, the first thing which Edward did after making his public entry into London was to proceed to the sanctuary to rejoin his wife, and deliver her from her duress, and also to see his new-born son.

Henry again sent to the Tower.

Queen Margaret was out of the kingdom at this time, being on a visit to the Continent. She had her son, the Prince of Wales, with her; but Henry, the king, was in London. He, of course, fell into Edward's hands, and was immediately sent back a prisoner to the Tower.

Edward remained only a day or two in London, and then set off again, at the head of all his troops, to meet Warwick. He brought out

King Henry from the Tower, and took him with the army as a prisoner.

Warwick refuses to yield.
Preparations for a battle.

Warwick had now strengthened himself so far that he was prepared for battle. The two armies approached each other not many miles from London. Before commencing hostilities, Clarence wished for an opportunity to attempt a reconciliation; he, of course, felt a strong desire to make peace, if possible, for his situation, in case of battle, would be painful in the extreme—his brothers on one side, and his father-in-law on the other, and he himself compelled to fight against the cause which he had abandoned and betrayed. So he sent a messenger to the earl, offering to act as mediator between him and his brother, in hopes of finding some mode of arranging the quarrel; but the earl, instead of accepting the mediation, sent back only invectives and defiance.

"Go tell your master," he said to the messenger, "that Warwick is not the man to follow the example of faithlessness and treason which the false, perjured Clarence has set him. Unlike him, I stand true to my oath, and this quarrel can only be settled by the sword."

Of course, nothing now remained but to fight the battle, and a most desperate and bloody battle it was. It was fought upon a plain at a place called Barnet. It lasted from four in the morning till ten.

DEATH OF WARWICK ON THE FIELD OF BARNET

Richard came forward in the fight in a very conspicuous and prominent manner. He was now about eighteen years of age, and this was the first serious battle in which he had been actually engaged. He evinced a great deal of heroism, and won great praise by the ardor in which he rushed into the thickest of the fight, and by the manner in which he conducted himself there. The squires who attended him were both killed, but Richard himself remained unhurt.

Edward victorious.
Warwick slain.

In the end, Edward was victorious. The quarrel was thus decided by the sword, as Warwick had said, and decided, so far as the earl was concerned, terribly and irrevocably, for he himself was unhorsed upon the field, and slain. Many thousands of soldiers fell on each side, and great numbers of the leading nobles. The bodies were buried in one common trench, which was dug for the purpose on the plain, and a chapel was afterward erected over them, to mark and consecrate the spot.

King Henry.

It is said in respect to King Henry, who had been taken from the Tower and made to accompany the army to the field, that Edward placed him in the midst of the fight at Barnet, in the hope that he might in this way be slain, either by accident or design. This plan, however, if it were formed, did not succeed, for Henry escaped unharmed, and, after the battle, was taken back to London, and again conveyed through the gloomy streets of the lower city to his solitary prison in the Tower. The streets were filled, after he had passed, with groups of men of all ranks and stations, discussing the strange and mournful vicissitudes in the life of this hapless monarch, now for the second time cut off from all his friends, and immured hopelessly in a dismal dungeon.

Margaret and the Prince of Wales.
On the very day of the battle of Barnet, Queen Margaret, who had hastened her return to England on hearing of Edward's invasion, landed at Plymouth, in the southwestern part of England. The young Prince of Wales, her son, was with her. When she heard the terrible tidings of the loss of the battle of Barnet and the death of Warwick, she was struck with consternation, and immediately fled to an abbey in the neighborhood of the place where she had landed,

and took sanctuary there. She soon, however, recovered from this panic, and came forth again. She put herself, with her son, at the head of the French troops which she had brought with her, and collected also as many more as she could induce to join her, and then, marching slowly toward the northward, finally took a strong position on the River Severn, near the town of Tewkesbury. Tewkesbury is in the western part of England, near the frontiers of Wales.

STREET LEADING TO THE TOWER

Meeting of the armies.

Edward, having received intelligence of her movements, collected his forces also, and, accompanied by Clarence and Gloucester, went forth to meet her. The two armies met about three weeks after the battle of Barnet, in which Warwick was killed. All the flower of the English nobility were there, on one side or on the other.

Two boys to command.

Queen Margaret's son, the Prince of Wales, was now about eighteen years of age, and his mother placed him in command—nominally at the head of the army. Edward, on his side, assigned the same position to Richard, who was almost precisely of the same age with the Prince of Wales. Thus the great and terrible battle which ensued was fought, as it were, by two boys, cousins to each other, and neither of them out of their teens.

The killing of Lord Wenlock.

The operations were, however, really directed by older and more experienced men. The chief counselor on Margaret's side was the Duke of Somerset. Edward's army attempted, by means of certain evolutions, to entice the queen's army out of their camp. Somerset wished to go, and he commanded the men to follow. Some followed, but others remained behind. Among those that remained behind was a body of men under the command of a certain Lord Wenlock. Somerset was angry because they did not follow him, and he suspected, moreover, that Lord Wenlock was intending to betray the queen and go over to the other side; so he turned back in a rage, and, coming up to Lord Wenlock, struck him a dreadful blow upon his helmet with his battle-axe, and killed him on the spot.

End of the battle.

In the midst of the confusion which this affair produced, Richard, at the head of his brother's troops, came forcing his way into the intrenchments, bearing down all before him. The queen's army was thrown into confusion, and put to flight. Thousands upon thousands were killed. As many as could save themselves from being slaughtered upon the spot fled into the country toward the north, pursued by detached parties of their enemies.

The young Prince of Wales was taken prisoner. The queen fled, and for a time it was not known what had become of her. She fled to the church in Tewkesbury, and took refuge there.

CHURCH AT TEWKESBURY

Murder of the Prince of Wales.

As for the Prince of Wales, the account of his fate which was given at the time, and has generally been believed since, is this: As soon as the battle was over, he was brought, disarmed and helpless, into King Edward's tent, and there Edward, Clarence, Gloucester, and others gathered around to triumph over him, and taunt him with his downfall. Edward came up to him, and, after gazing upon him a moment in a fierce and defiant manner, demanded of him, in a furious tone, "What brought him to England?"

"My father's crown and my own inheritance," replied the prince.

Edward uttered some exclamation of anger, and then struck the prince upon the mouth with his gauntlet.[5]

At this signal, Gloucester, and the others who were standing by, fell upon the poor helpless boy, and killed him on the spot. The prince cried to Clarence, who was his brother-in-law, to save him, but in vain; Clarence did not interfere.

Some of the modern defenders of Richard's character attempt to show that there is no sufficient evidence that this story is true, and they maintain that the prince was slain upon the field, after the battle, and that Richard was innocent of his death. The evidence, however, seems strongly against this last supposition.

The queen's refuge.

Soon after the battle, it was found that the queen, with her attendants, as has already been stated, had taken refuge in a church at Tewkesbury, and in other sacred structures near.

Edward in the church.

Edward proceeded directly to the church, with the intention of hunting out his enemies wherever he could find them. He broke into the sacred precincts, sword in hand, attended by a number of reckless and desperate followers, and would have slain those that had taken refuge there, on the spot, had not the abbot himself come forward and interposed to protect them. He came dressed in his sacerdotal robes, and bearing the sacred emblems in his hands.

---

[5] The gauntlet was a sort of iron glove, the fingers of which were made flexible by joints formed with scales sliding over each other.

These emblems he held up before the infuriated Edward as a token of the sanctity of the place. By these means the king's hand was stayed, and, before allowing him to go away, the abbot exacted from him a promise that he would molest the refugees no more.

QUEEN MARGARET BROUGHT IN PRISONER AT COVENTRY

This promise was, however, not made to be kept. Two days afterward Edward appointed a court-martial, and sent Richard, with an armed force, to the church, to take all the men that had sought refuge there, and bring them out for trial. The trial was conducted with very little ceremony, and the men were all beheaded on the green, in Tewkesbury, that very day.

Margaret taken.

Queen Margaret and the ladies who attended her were not with them. They had sought refuge in another place. They were, however, found after a few days, and were all brought prisoners to Edward's camp at Coventry; for, after the battle, Edward had begun to move on with his army across the country.

Conducted a prisoner to London.

The king's first idea was to send Margaret immediately to London and put her in the Tower; but, before he did this, a change in his plans took place, which led him to decide to go to London himself. So he took Queen Margaret with him, a captive in his train. On the arrival of the party in London, the queen was conveyed at once to the Tower.

74

Here she remained a close prisoner for five long and weary years, and was then ransomed by the King of France and taken to the Continent. She lived after this in comparative obscurity for about ten years, and then died.

Henry is put to death in the Tower.

As for her husband, his earthly troubles were brought to an end much sooner. The cause of the change of plan above referred to, which led Edward to go directly to London soon after the battle of Tewkesbury, was the news that a relative of Warwick, whom that nobleman, during his lifetime, had put in command in the southeastern part of England, had raised an insurrection there, with a view of marching to London, rescuing Henry from the Tower, and putting him upon the throne. This movement was soon put down, and Edward returned from the expedition triumphant to London. He and his brothers spent the night after their arrival in the Tower. The next morning King Henry was found dead in his bed.

The universal belief was then, and has been since, that he was put to death by Edward's orders, and it has been the general opinion that Richard was the murderer.

The body of the king was put upon a bier that same day, and conveyed to St. Paul's Church in London, and there exhibited to the public for a long time, with guards and torch-bearers surrounding it. An immense concourse of people came to view his remains. The object of this exposition of the body of the king was to make sure the fact of his death in the public mind, and prevent the possibility of the circulation of rumors, subsequently, by the partisans of his house, that he was still alive; for such rumors would greatly have increased the danger of any insurrectionary plans which might be formed against Edward's authority.

Burial of Henry VI.

In due time the body was interred at Windsor, and a sculptured monument, adorned with various arms and emblems, was erected over the tomb.

The Lancastrian party completely subdued.

The remaining leaders on the Lancaster side were disposed of in a very effectual manner, to prevent the possibility of their again acquiring power. Some were banished. Others were shut up in various castles as hopeless prisoners. The country was thus wholly subdued, and Edward was once more established firmly on his throne.

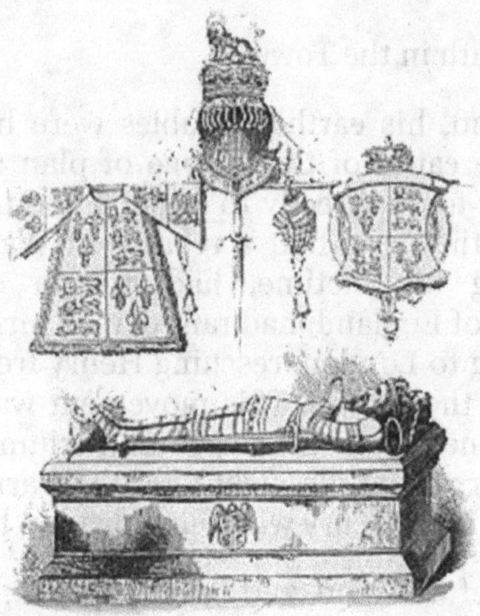

TOMB OF HENRY VI

1471-1474

Characters of Clarence and Richard.

When the affairs of the kingdom were settled, after the return of King Edward to the throne, Richard, Duke of Gloucester, the subject of the present volume, was found occupying a very exalted and brilliant position. It is true, he was yet very young, being only about nineteen years of age, and by birth he was second to Clarence, Clarence being his older brother. But Clarence had been so wavering and vacillating, having changed sides so often in the great quarrels, that no confidence was placed in him now on either side. Richard, on the other hand, had steadily adhered to his brother Edward's cause. He had shared all his brother's reverses, and he had rendered him most valuable and efficient aid in all the battles which he had fought, and had contributed essentially to his success in all the victories which he had gained. Of course, now, Edward and his friends had great confidence in Richard, while Clarence was looked upon with suspicion and distrust.

Embarrassing situation in which Clarence was placed.

Clarence, it is true, had one excuse for his instability, which Richard had not; for Clarence, having married the Earl of Warwick's daughter, was, of course, brought into very close connection with the earl, and was subjected greatly to his influence. Accordingly, whatever course Warwick decided to take, it was extremely difficult for Clarence to avoid joining him in it; and when at length Warwick arranged the marriage of his daughter Anne with the Prince of Wales, King Henry's son, and so joined himself to the Lancaster party, Clarence was placed between two strong and contrary attractions—his attachment to his brother, and his natural interest in the advancement of his own family being on one side, and his love for his wife, and the great influence and ascendency exerted over his mind by his father-in-law being on the other.

Richard was in no such strait. There was nothing to entice him away from his fidelity to his brother, so he remained true.

He had been so brave and efficient, too, in the military operations connected with Edward's recovery of the throne, that he had acquired great renown as a soldier throughout the kingdom. The fame of his exploits was the more brilliant on account of his youth. It was considered remarkable that a young man not yet out of his teens should show so much skill, and act with so much resolution and energy in times so trying, and the country resounded with his praises.

Richard made Lord High Admiral of England.

As soon as Edward was established on the throne, he raised Richard to what was in those days, perhaps, the highest office under the crown, that of Lord High Admiral of England. This was the office which the Earl of Warwick had held, and to which a great portion of the power and influence which he exercised was owing. The Lord High Admiral had command of the navy, and of the principal ports on both sides of the English Channel, so long as any ports on the French side remained in English hands. The reader will recollect, perhaps, that while Richard was quite a small boy, his mother was compelled to fly with him and his little brother George to France, to escape from the enemies of the family, at the time of his father's death, and that it was through the Earl of Warwick's co-operation that she was enabled to accomplish this flight. Now it was in consequence of Warwick's being at that time Lord High Admiral of England, and his having command of Calais, and the waters between Calais and England, that he could make arrangements to assist Lady Cecily so effectually on that occasion.

His real character.
Requisites of a good soldier.

Still, Richard, though universally applauded for his military courage and energy, was known to all who had opportunities of becoming personally acquainted with him to be a bad man. He was unprincipled, hard-hearted, and reckless. This, however, did not detract from his military fame. Indeed, depravity of private character seldom diminishes much the applause which a nation bestows upon those who acquire military renown in their service. It is not to be expected that it should. Military exploits have been, in fact, generally, in the history of the world, gigantic crimes, committed by reckless and remorseless men for the benefit of others, who, though they would be deterred by their scruples of conscience or their moral sensibilities from perpetrating such deeds themselves, are ready to repay, with the most extravagant honors and rewards, those who are ferocious and unscrupulous enough to perpetrate them in their stead. Were it not for some very few and rare exceptions to the general rule, which have from time to time appeared, the history of mankind would show that, to be a *good soldier*, it is almost absolutely essential to be a *bad man*.

Young Edward formally acknowledged heir to the crown.

The child, Prince Edward, the son of Edward the Fourth, who was born, as is related in a preceding chapter, in the sanctuary at Westminster, whither his mother had fled at the time when Edward was expelled from the kingdom, was, of course, King Edward's heir. He was now less than a year old, and, in order to place his title to the crown beyond dispute, a solemn oath was required from all the leading nobles and officers of Edward's government, that in case he survived his father they would acknowledge him as king. The following is the form of the oath which was taken:

I acknowledge, take, and repute you, Edward, Prince of Wales, Duke of Cornwayll, and Erl of Chestre, furste begoten son of oure sovereigne lord, as to the corones and reames of England and of France, and lordship of Ireland; and promette and swere that in case hereafter it happen you by Goddis disposition do outlive our sovereigne lord, I shall then take and accept you for true, veray and righteous King of England, and of France, and of Ireland; and feith and trouth to you shall here, and yn all thyngs truely and feithfully behave me towardes you and youre heyres, as a true and feithful subject oweth to behave him to his sovereigne lord and righteous King of England, France, and Ireland; so help me God, and Holidome, and this holy Evangelist.

Richard took this oath with the rest. How he kept it will hereafter appear.

Forlorn condition of Lady Anne.

The Lady Anne, the second daughter of the Earl of Warwick, who had been betrothed to the Prince of Wales, King Henry's son, was left, by the fall of the house of Lancaster and the re-establishment of King Edward the Fourth upon the throne, in a most forlorn and pitiable condition. Her father, the earl, was dead, having been killed in battle. Her betrothed husband, too, the Prince of Wales, with whom she had fondly hoped one day to sit on the throne of England, had been cruelly assassinated. Queen Margaret, the mother of the prince, who might have been expected to take an interest in her fate, was a helpless prisoner in the Tower. And if the fallen queen had been at liberty, it is very probable that all her interest in Anne would prove to have been extinguished by the death of her son; for Queen Margaret had never felt any personal preference for Anne, and had only consented to the marriage very reluctantly, and from political considerations alone. The friends and connections of her father's family, a short time since so exalted in station and so powerful, were now scattered and destroyed. Some had been killed in battle, others beheaded by executioners, others banished from the realm. The rest were roaming about England in terror and distress, houseless, homeless, friendless, and only intent to find some hiding-place where they might screen themselves from Edward's power and vengeance.

Her sister Isabella.

There was one exception, indeed, the Lady Isabella, Clarence's wife, who, as the reader will recollect, was Warwick's oldest daughter, and, of course, the sister of Lady Anne. She and Clarence, her husband, it might be supposed, would take an interest in Lady Anne's fate. Indeed, Clarence did take an interest in it, but, unfortunately, the interest was of the wrong kind.

Clarence's views in respect to the property.

The Earl of Warwick had been immensely wealthy. Besides the ancient stronghold of the family, Warwick Castle, one of the most renowned old feudal fortresses in England, he owned many other castles, and many large estates, and rights of property of various kinds all over the kingdom. Now Clarence, after Warwick's death, had taken most of this property into his own hands as the husband of the earl's oldest daughter, and he wished to keep it. This he could easily do while Anne remained in her present friendless and helpless condition. But he knew very well that if she were to be married to any person of rank and influence on the York side, her husband would insist on a division of the property. Now he suspected that his brother Richard had conceived the design of marrying her. He accordingly set himself at work earnestly to thwart this design.

Richard's plan.

It was true that Richard had conceived the idea of making Anne his wife, from the motive, however, solely, as it would seem, to obtain her share of her father's property.

His early acquaintance with Anne.

Richard had been acquainted with Anne from her childhood. Indeed, he was related to the family of the Earl of Warwick on his mother's side. His mother, Lady Cecily Neville, belonged to the same great family of Neville from which the Warwicks sprung. Warwick had been a great friend of Lady Cecily in former years, and it is even supposed that when Richard and his brother George were brought back from the Continent, at the time when Edward first obtained possession of the kingdom, they lived for a time in Warwick's family at Middleham Castle. This is not quite certainly known, but it is at any rate known that Richard and Anne knew each other well when they were children, and were often together.

The banquet at the archbishop's.

There is an account of a grand entertainment which was given by the Warwick family at York, some years before, on the occasion of the enthroning of the earl's brother George as Archbishop of York, at which Richard was present. Richard, being a prince of the blood royal, was, of course, a very highly honored guest, notwithstanding that he was but a child. So they prepared for him and some few other great personages a raised platform, called a dais, at one end of the banquet-hall, with a royal canopy over it. The table for the distinguished personages was upon this dais, while those for the other guests extended up and down the hall below. Richard was seated at the centre of the table of honor, with a countess on one side of him and a duchess on the other. Opposite to him, at the same table, were seated Isabella and Anne. Anne was at this time about twelve years old.

Now it is supposed that Isabella and Anne were placed at this table to please Richard, for their mother, who was, of course, entitled to take precedence of them, had her seat at one of the large tables below.

From this and some other similar indications, it is supposed that Richard took a fancy to Anne while they were quite young, as Clarence did to Isabella. Indeed, one of the ancient writers says that Richard wished, at this early period, to choose her for his wife, but that she did not like him.

Clarence conceals Lady Anne.

At any rate, now, after the re-establishment of his brother upon the throne, and his own exaltation to such high office under him, he determined that he would marry Anne. Clarence, on the other hand, determined that he should not marry her. So Clarence, with the pretense of taking her under his protection, seized her, and carried her away to a place of concealment, where he kept her closely shut up. Anne consented to this, for she wished to keep out of Richard's way. Richard's person was disagreeable to her, and his character was hateful. She seems to have considered him, as he is generally represented by the writers of those times, as a rude, hard-hearted, and unscrupulous man; and she had also a special reason for shrinking from him with horror, as the mortal enemy of her father, and the reputed murderer of the husband to whom she had been betrothed.

Richard finds her at last.

Clarence kept her for some time in obscure places of concealment, changing the place from time to time to elude the vigilance of Richard, who was continually making search for her. The poor princess had recourse to all manner of contrivances, and assumed the most humble disguises to keep herself concealed, and was at last reduced to a very forlorn and destitute condition, through the desperate shifts that she resorted to, in her endeavors to escape Richard's persecutions. All was, however, in vain. Richard discovered her at last in a mean house in London, where she was living in the disguise of a servant. He immediately seized her, and conveyed her to a place of security which was under his control.

Soon after this she was taken away from this place and conveyed to York, and placed, for the time, under the protection of the archbishop—the same archbishop at whose enthronement, eight or ten years before, she had sat at the same table with Richard, under the royal canopy. But she was not left at peace here. Richard insisted on her marrying him. She insisted on her refusal. Her friends—the few that she had left—turned against her, and urged her to consent to the union; but she could not endure the thought of it.

His marriage.
Measures for securing the property.

Richard, however, persisted in his determination, and Anne was finally overcome. It is said she resisted to the last, and that the ceremony was performed by compulsion, Anne continuing to refuse her consent to the end. It was foreseen that, as soon as any change of circumstances should enable her to resume active resistance to the union, she would repudiate the marriage altogether, as void for want of her consent, or else obtain a divorce. To guard against this danger, Richard procured the passage of an act of Parliament, by which he was empowered to continue in the full possession and enjoyment of Anne's property, even if *she were to divorce him*, provided that he did his best to be reconciled to her, and was willing to be re-married to her, with her consent, whenever she was willing to grant it.

RICHARD III

QUEEN ANNE

Difficulty about the division of the property.

As for Richard himself, his object was fully attained by the accomplishment of a marriage so far acknowledged as to entitle him to the possession of the property of his wife. There was still some difficulty, however, arising from a disagreement between Richard and Clarence in respect to the division. Clarence, when he found that Richard would marry Anne, in spite of all that he could do to prevent it, declared, with an oath, that, even if Richard did marry her, he, Clarence, would never "part the livelihood," that is, divide the property with him.

The quarrel becomes serious.
It is at last settled by the king.

So fixed was Clarence in this resolution to retain all the property himself, and so resolute was Richard, on the other hand, in his determination to have his share, that the quarrel very soon assumed a very serious character. The lords and nobles of the court took part in the controversy on one side and on the other, until, at length, there was imminent danger of open war. Finally Edward himself interposed, and summoned the brothers to appear before him in open council, when, after a full hearing of the dispute, he said that he himself would decide the question. Accordingly, the two brothers appeared before the king, and each strenuously argued his own cause. The king, after hearing them, decided how the property should be divided. He gave to Richard and Anne a large share, but not all that Richard claimed. Richard was, however, compelled to submit.

MIDDLEHAM CASTLE

When the marriage was thus consummated, and Richard had been put in possession of his portion of the property, Anne seems to have submitted to her fate, and she went with Richard to Middleham Castle, in the north of England. This castle was one which had belonged to the Warwick family, and it now came into Richard's possession. Richard did not, however, remain long here with his wife. He went away on various military expeditions, leaving Anne most of the time alone. She was well contented to be thus left, for nothing could be so welcome to her now as to be relieved as much as possible from the presence of her hateful husband.

Richard's child is born.
Anne becomes more contented.

This state of things continued, without much change, until the end of about a year after her marriage, when Anne gave birth to a son.

The boy was named Edward. The possession of this treasure awakened in the breast of Anne a new interest in life, and repaid her, in some measure, for the sorrows and sufferings which she had so long endured.

Her love for her babe, in fact, awakened in her heart something like a tie to bind her to her husband. It is hard for a mother to continue long to hate the father of her child.

A.D. 1475–1483

Richard's high position.

King Edward reigned, after this time, for about eight years. During this period, Richard continued to occupy a very high official position, and a very conspicuous place in the public mind. He was generally considered as personally a very bad man, and, whenever any great public crime was committed, in which the government were implicated at all, it was Richard, usually, who was supposed to be chiefly instrumental in the perpetration of it; but, notwithstanding this, his fame, and the general consideration in which he was held, were very high. This was owing, in a considerable degree, to his military renown, and the straightforward energy and decision which characterized all his doings.

His character.

He generally co-operated very faithfully in all Edward's plans and schemes, though sometimes, when he thought them calculated to impede rather than promote the interests of the kingdom and the aggrandizement of the family, he made no secret of opposing them. As to Clarence, no one placed any trust or confidence in him whatever. For a time, he and Edward were ostensibly on friendly terms with each other, but there was no cordial good-will between them. Each watched the other with continual suspicion and distrust.

Edward's plan for the invasion of France.

About the year 1475, Edward formed a grand scheme for the invasion of France, in order to recover from the French king certain possessions which Edward claimed, on the ground of their having formerly belonged to his ancestors. This plan, as, indeed, almost all plans of war and conquest were in those days, was very popular in England, and arrangements were made on an immense scale for fitting out an expedition. The Duke of Burgundy, who, as will be recollected, had married Edward's sister, promised to join the English in this proposed war. When all was ready, the English army set sail, and crossed over to Calais. Edward went with the army as commander-in-chief. He was accompanied by Clarence and

Gloucester. Thus far every thing had gone on well, and all Europe was watching with great interest for the result of the expedition; but, very soon after landing, great difficulties arose. The Duke of Burgundy and Edward disagreed, and this disagreement caused great delays. The army advanced slowly toward the French frontier, but for two months nothing effectual was done.

LOUIS XI. OF FRANCE

Character of King Louis.
Louis's wily management.
Treaty proposed.

In the mean time, Louis, the King of France, who was a very shrewd and wily man, concluded that it would be better for him to buy off his enemies than to fight them. So he continually sent messengers and negotiators to Edward's camp with proposals of various sorts, made to gain time, in order to enable him, by means of presents and bribes, to buy up all the prominent leaders and counselors of the expedition. He gave secretly to all the men who he supposed held an influence over Edward's mind, large sums of money. He offered, too, to make a treaty with Edward, by which, under one pretext or another, he was to pay him a great deal of money. One of these proposed payments was that of a large sum for the ransom of Queen Margaret, as mentioned in a preceding chapter. The amount of the ransom money which he proposed was fifty thousand crowns.

Besides these promises to pay money in case the treaty was concluded, Louis made many rich and valuable presents at once.

One day, while the negotiations were pending, he sent over to the English camp, as a gift to the king, three hundred cart-loads of wine, the best that could be procured in the kingdom.

At one time, near the beginning of the affair, when a herald was sent to Louis from Edward with a very defiant and insolent message, Louis, instead of resenting the message as an affront, entertained the herald with great politeness, held a long and friendly conversation with him, and finally sent him away with three hundred crowns in his purse, and a promise of a thousand more as soon as a peace should be concluded. He also made him a present of a piece of crimson velvet "thirty ells long." Such a gift as this of the crimson velvet was calculated, perhaps, in those days of military foppery, to please the herald even more than the money.

These things, of course, put Edward and nearly all his followers in excellent humor, and disposed them to listen very favorably to any propositions for settling the quarrel which Louis might be disposed to make. At last, after various and long protracted negotiations, a treaty was agreed upon, and Louis proposed that at the final execution of it he and Edward should have a personal interview.

Edward acceded to this on certain conditions, and the circumstances under which the interview took place, and the arrangements which were adopted on the occasion, make it one of the most curious transactions of the whole reign.

Arrangements made for a personal interview.
The grating on the bridge.

It seems that Edward could not place the least trust in Louis's professions of friendship, and did not dare to meet him without requiring beforehand most extraordinary precautions to guard against the possibility of treachery. So it was agreed that the meeting should take place upon a bridge, Louis and his friends to come in upon one side of the bridge, and Edward, with his party, on the other. In order to prevent either party from seizing and carrying off the other, there was a strong barricade of wood built across the bridge in the middle of it, and the arrangement was for the King of France to come up to this barricade on one side, and the King of England on the other, and so shake hands and communicate with each other through the bars of the barricade.

The place where this most extraordinary royal meeting was held was called Picquigny, and the treaty which was made there is known in history as the Treaty of Picquigny. The town is on the River Somme, near the city of Amiens. Amiens was at that time very near the French frontier.

The day appointed for the meeting was the 29th of August, 1475. The barricade was prepared. It was made of strong bars, crossing each other so as to form a grating, such as was used in those days to make the cages of bears, and lions, and other wild beasts. The spaces between the bars were only large enough to allow a man's arm to pass through.

The King of France went first to the grating, advancing, of course, from the French side. He was accompanied by ten or twelve attendants, all men of high rank and station. He was very specially dressed for the occasion. The dress was made of cloth of gold, with a large *fleur de lis*—which was at that time the emblem of the French sovereignty—magnificently worked upon it in precious stones.

Meeting of the kings at the grating.

When Louis and his party had reached the barricade, Edward, attended likewise by his friends, approached on the other side. When they came to the barricade, the two kings greeted each other with many bows and other salutations, and they also shook hands with each other by reaching through the grating. The King of France addressed Edward in a very polite and courteous manner. "Cousin," said he, "you are right welcome. There is no person living that I have been so ambitious of seeing as you, and God be thanked that our interview now is on so happy an occasion."

After these preliminary salutations and ceremonies had been concluded, a prayer-book, or missal, as it was called, and a crucifix, were brought forward, and held at the grating where both kings could touch them. Each of the kings then put his hands upon them—one hand on the crucifix and the other on the missal—and they both took a solemn oath by these sacred emblems that they would faithfully keep the treaty which they had made.

Jocose conversation of the two kings.

After thus transacting the business which had brought them together, the two kings conversed with each other in a gay and merry manner for some time. The King of France invited Edward to come to Paris and make him a visit. This, of course, was a joke, for Edward would as soon think of accepting an invitation from a lion to come and visit him in his den, as of putting himself in Louis's power by going to Paris. Both monarchs and all the attendants laughed merrily at this jest. Louis assured Edward that he would have a very pleasant time at Paris in amusing himself with the gay ladies, and in other dissipations. "And then here is the cardinal," he added, turning to the Cardinal of Bourbon, an ecclesiastic of very high rank, but of very loose character, who was among his attendants, "who will grant you a very easy absolution for any sins you may take a fancy to commit while you are there."

Edward and his friends were much amused with this sportive conversation of Louis's, and Edward made many smart replies, especially joking the cardinal, who, he knew, "was a gay man with the ladies, and a boon companion over his wine."

This sort of conversation continued for some time, and at length the kings, after again shaking hands through the grating, departed each his own way, and thus this most extraordinary conference of sovereigns was terminated.

Terms of the treaty.

The treaty which was thus made at the bridge of Picquigny contained several very important articles. The principal of them were the following:

1. Louis was to pay fifty thousand crowns as a ransom for Queen Margaret, and Edward was to release her from the Tower and send her to France as soon as he arrived in England.

2. Louis was to pay to Edward in cash, on the spot, seventy-five thousand crowns, and an annuity of fifty thousand crowns.

Marriage agreed upon.

3. He was to marry his son, the dauphin, to Edward's oldest daughter, Elizabeth, and, in case of her death, then to his next daughter, Mary. These parties were all children at this time, and so the actual marriage was postponed for a time; but it was stipulated solemnly that it should be performed as soon as the prince and princess attained to a proper age. It is important to remember this part of the treaty, as a great and

serious difficulty grew out of it when the time for the execution of it arrived.

4. By the last article, the two kings bound themselves to a truce for seven years, during which time hostilities were to be entirely suspended, and free trade between the two countries was to be allowed.

Clarence and Gloucester.

Clarence was with the king at the time of making this treaty, and he joined with the other courtiers in giving it his approval, but Richard would have nothing to do with it. He very much preferred to go on with the war, and was indignant that his brother should allow himself to be bought off, as it were, by presents and payments of money, and induced to consent to what seemed to him an ignominious peace. He did not give any open expression to his discontent, but he refused to be present at the conference on the bridge, and, when Edward and the army, after the peace was concluded, went back to England, he went with them, but in very bad humor.

The people of England discontented.
The people of England were in very bad humor too. You will observe that the inducements which Louis employed in procuring the treaty were gifts and sums of money granted to Edward himself, and to his great courtiers personally for their own private uses. There was nothing in his concessions which tended at all to the aggrandizement or to the benefit of the English realm, or to promote the interest of the people at large. They thought, therefore, that Edward and his counselors had been induced to sacrifice the rights and honor of the crown and the kingdom to their own personal advantage by a system of gross and open bribery, and they were very much displeased.

Renewal of the quarrel between Edward and Clarence.
Clarence retires from court.

The next great event which marks the history of the reign of Edward, after the conclusion of this war, was the breaking out anew of the old feud between Edward and Clarence, and the dreadful crisis to which the quarrel finally reached. The renewal of the quarrel began in Edward's dispossessing Clarence of a portion of his property. Edward was very much embarrassed for money after his return from the French expedition. He had incurred great debts in fitting out the expedition, and these debts the Parliament and people of England were very unwilling to pay, on account of their being so much displeased with the peace which had been made. Edward, consequently, notwithstanding the bribes which he had received from Louis, was very much in want of money. At last he caused a law to be passed by Parliament enacting that all the patrimony of the royal family, which had hitherto been divided among the three brothers, should be resumed, and applied to the service of the crown. This made Clarence very angry. True, he was extremely rich, through the property which he had received by his wife from the Warwick estates, but this did not make him any more willing to submit patiently to be robbed by his brother. He expressed his anger very openly, and the ill feeling which the affair occasioned led to a great many scenes of dispute and crimination between the two brothers, until at last Clarence could no longer endure to have any thing to do with Edward, and he went away, with Isabella his wife, to a castle which he possessed near Tewkesbury, and there remained, in angry and sullen seclusion. So great was the animosity that prevailed at this time between the brothers and their respective partisans, that almost every one who took an active part in the quarrel lived in continual anxiety from fear of being poisoned, or of being destroyed by incantations or witchcraft.

Belief in witchcraft.

Every body believed in witchcraft in these days. There was one peculiar species of necromancy which was held in great dread. It was supposed that certain persons had the power secretly to destroy any one against whom they conceived a feeling of ill will in the following manner: They would first make an effigy of their intended victim out of wax and other similar materials. This image was made the representation of the person to be destroyed by means of certain sorceries and incantations, and then it was by slow degrees, from day to day, melted away and gradually destroyed. While the image was thus melting, the innocent and unconscious victim of the witchcraft would pine away, and at last, when the image was fairly gone, would die.

Birth of Clarence's second son.

Not very long after Clarence left the court and went to Tewkesbury, his wife gave birth to a child. It was the second son. The child was named Richard, and is known in history as Richard of Clarence. Isabella did not recover her health and strength after the birth of her child. She pined away in a slow and lingering manner for two or three months, and then died.

Clarence was convinced that she did not die a natural death. He believed that her life had been destroyed by some process of witchcraft, such as has been described, or by poison, and he openly charged the queen with having instigated the murder by having employed some sorcerer or assassin to accomplish it. After a time he satisfied himself that a certain woman named Ankaret Twynhyo was the person whom the queen had employed to commit this crime, and watching an opportunity when this woman was at her own residence, away from all who could protect her, he sent a body of armed men from among his retainers, who went secretly to the place, and, breaking in suddenly, seized the woman and bore her off to Warwick Castle. There Clarence subjected her to what he called a trial, and she was condemned to death, and executed at once. The charge against her was that she administered poison to the duchess in a cup of ale. So summary were these proceedings, that the poor woman was dead in three hours from the time that she arrived at the castle gates.

These proceedings, of course, greatly exasperated Edward and the queen, and made them hate Clarence more than ever.

New quarrels.
The rich heiress.

Very soon after this, Charles, the Duke of Burgundy, who married Margaret, Edward and Clarence's sister, and who had been Edward's ally in so many of his wars, was killed in battle. He left a daughter named Mary, of whom Margaret was the step-mother; for Mary was the child of the duke by a former marriage. Now, as Charles was possessed of immense estates, Mary, by his death, became a great heiress, and Clarence, now that his wife was dead, conceived the idea of making her his second wife. He immediately commenced negotiations to this end. Margaret favored the plan, but Edward and Elizabeth, the queen, as soon as they heard of it, set themselves at work in the most earnest manner to thwart and circumvent it.

Edward and Clarence quarrel about the heiress.

Their motives for opposing this match arose partly from their enmity to Clarence, and partly from designs of their own which they had formed in respect to the marriage of Mary. The queen wished to secure the young heiress for one of her brothers. Edward had another plan, which was to marry Mary to a certain Duke Maximilian. Edward's plan, in the end, was carried out, and Clarence was defeated. When Clarence found at length that the bride, with all the immense wealth and vastly increased importance which his marriage with her was to bring, were lost to him through Edward's interference, and conferred upon his hated rival Maximilian, he was terribly enraged. He expressed his resentment and anger against the king in the most violent terms.

About this time a certain nobleman, one of the king's friends, died. The king accused a priest, who was in Clarence's service, of having killed him by sorcery. The priest was seized and put to the torture to compel him to confess his crime and to reveal his confederates. The priest at length confessed, and named as his accomplice one of Clarence's household named Burdett, a gentleman who lived in very intimate and confidential relations with Clarence himself.

The confession was taken as proof of guilt, and the priest and Burdett were both immediately executed.

Clarence becomes furious.

Clarence was now perfectly frantic with rage. He could restrain himself no longer. He forced his way into the king's council-chamber, and there uttered to the lords who were assembled the most violent and angry denunciation of the king. He accused him of injustice and cruelty, and upbraided him, and all who counseled and aided him, in the severest terms.

He is sent to the Tower.

When the king, who was not himself present on this occasion, heard what Clarence had done, he said that such proceedings were subversive of the laws of the realm, and destructive to all good government, and he commanded that Clarence should be arrested and sent to the Tower.

Clarence is accused of high treason.

After a short time the king summoned a Parliament, and when the assembly was convened, he brought his brother out from his prison in the Tower, and arraigned him at the bar of the House of Lords on charges of the most extraordinary character, which he himself personally preferred against him. In these charges Clarence was accused of having formed treasonable conspiracies to depose the king, disinherit the king's children, and raise himself to the throne, and with this view of having slandered the king, and endeavored, by bribes and false representations, to entice away his subjects from their allegiance; of having joined himself with the Lancastrian faction so far as to promise to restore them their estates which had been confiscated, provided that they would assist him in usurping the throne; and of having secretly organized an armed force, which was all ready, and waiting only for the proper occasion to strike the blow.

Clarence denied all these charges in the most earnest and solemn manner. The king insisted upon the truth of them, and brought forward many witnesses to prove them. Of course, whether the charges were true or false, there could be no difficulty in finding plenty of witnesses to give the required testimony. The lords listened to the charges and the defense with a sort of solemn awe. Indeed, all England, as it were, stood by, silenced and appalled at the progress of this dreadful fraternal quarrel, and at the prospect of the terrible termination of it, which all could foresee must come.

THE MURDERERS COMING FOR CLARENCE

He is sentenced to death.

Whatever the members of Parliament may have thought of the truth or falsehood of the charges, there was only one way in which it was prudent or even safe for them to vote, and Clarence was condemned to death.

Sentence being passed, the prisoner was remanded to the Tower.

He is assassinated.

Edward seems, after all, to have shrunk from the open and public execution of the sentence which he had caused to be pronounced against his brother. No public execution took place, but in a short time it was announced that Clarence had died in prison. It was understood that assassins were employed to go privately into the room where he was confined and put him to death; and it is universally believed, though there is no positive proof of the fact, that Richard was the person who made the arrangements for the performance of this deed.[6]

Dissipation and wickedness of Edward.

After Clarence was dead, and the excitement and anger of the quarrel had subsided in Edward's mind, he was overwhelmed with remorse and anguish at what he had done. He attempted to drown these painful thoughts by dissipation and vice. He neglected the affairs of his government, and his duties to his wife and family, and spent his time in gay pleasures with the ladies of his court, and in guilty carousings with wicked men. In these pleasures he spent large sums of money, wasting his patrimony and all his resources in extravagance and folly. Among other amusements, he used to form hunting-parties, in which the ladies of his court were accustomed to join, and he used to set up gay silken tents for their accommodation on the hunting-ground. He spent vast sums, too, upon his dress, being very vain of his personal attractions, and of the favor in which he was held by the ladies around him.

Jane Shore.

The most conspicuous of his various female favorites was the celebrated Jane Shore. She was the wife of a respectable citizen of London. Edward enticed her away from her husband, and induced her to come and live at court with him. The opposite engraving, which is taken from an ancient portrait, gives undoubtedly a correct representation both of her features and of her dress. We shall hear more of this person in the sequel.

---

[6] There was a strange story in respect to the manner of Clarence's death, which was very current at the time, namely, that he was drowned by his brothers in a butt of Malmsey wine. But there is no evidence whatever that this story was true.

JANE SHORE

Edward sends Richard to war.

Things went on in this way for about two years, when at length war broke out on the frontiers of Scotland. Edward was too much engrossed with his gallantries and pleasures to march himself to meet the enemy, and so he commissioned Richard to go. Richard was very well pleased that his brother Edward should remain at home, and waste away in effeminacy and vice his character and his influence in the kingdom, while he went forth in command of the army, to acquire, by the vigor and success of his military career, that ascendency that Edward was losing. So he took the command of the army and went forth to the war.

Difficulties in Scotland.

The war was protracted for several years. The King of Scotland had a brother, the Duke of Albany, who was attempting to dethrone him, in order that he might reign in his stead; that is, he was doing exactly that which Edward had charged upon his brother Clarence, and for which he had caused Clarence to be killed; and yet, with strange inconsistency, Edward espoused the cause of this Clarence of Scotland, and laid deep plans for enabling him to depose and supplant his brother.

In the midst of the measures which Richard was taking for the execution of these plans, they, as well as all Edward's other earthly schemes and hopes, were suddenly destroyed by the hand of death. Edward's health had become much impaired by the dissolute life which he had led, and at last he fell seriously sick. While he was sick, an affair occurred which vexed and worried his mind beyond endurance.

The reader will recollect that, at the treaty which Edward made with Louis of France at the barricade on the bridge of Picquigny, a marriage contract was concluded between Louis's oldest son, the Dauphin of France, and Edward's daughter Mary, and it was agreed that, as soon as the children were grown up, and were old enough, they should be married. Louis took a solemn oath upon the prayer-book and crucifix that he would not fail to keep this agreement.

But now some years had passed away, and circumstances had changed so much that Louis did not wish to keep this promise. Edward's great ally, the Duke of Burgundy, was dead. His daughter Mary, who became the Duchess Mary on the death of her father, and who, so greatly to Clarence's disappointment, had married Maximilian, had succeeded to the estates and possessions of her father. These possessions the King of France desired very much to join to his dominions, as they lay contiguous to them, and the fear of Edward, which had prompted him to make the marriage contract with him in the first instance, had now passed away, on account of Edward's having become so much weakened by his vices and his effeminacy. He now, therefore, became desirous of allying his family to that of Burgundy rather than that of England.

The Duchess Mary had three children, all very young. The oldest, Philip, was only about three years old.

Now it happened that just at this time, while the Duchess Mary was out with a small party, hawking, near the city of Bruges, as they were flying the hawks at some herons, the company galloping on over the fields in order to keep up with the birds, the duchess's horse, in taking a leap, burst the girths of the saddle, and the duchess was thrown off against the trunk of a tree. She was immediately taken up and borne into a house, but she was so much injured that she almost immediately died.

Louis's treachery.

Of course, her titles and estates would now descend to her children. The second of the children was a girl. Her name was Margaret. She was about two years old. Louis immediately resolved to give up the match between the dauphin and Edward's daughter Mary, and contract another alliance for him with this little Margaret. He met with considerable difficulty and delay in bringing this about, but he succeeded at last. While the negotiations were pending, Edward, who suspected what was going on, was assured that nothing of the kind was intended, and various false tales and pretenses were advanced by Louis to quiet his mind.

Vexation and rage of Edward.

At length, when all was settled, the new plan was openly proclaimed, and great celebrations and parades were held in Paris in honor of the event. Edward was overwhelmed with vexation and rage when he received the tidings. He was, however, completely helpless. He lay tossing restlessly on his sick-bed, cursing, on the one hand, Louis's faithlessness and treachery, and, on the other, his own miserable weakness and pain, which made it so utterly impossible that he should do any thing to resent the affront.

His death.

His vexation and rage so disturbed and worried him that they hastened his death. When he found that his last hour was drawing near, a new source of agitation and anguish was opened in his mind by the remorse which now began to overwhelm him for his vices and crimes. Long-forgotten deeds of injustice, of violence, and of every species of wickedness rose before his mind, and terrified him with awful premonition of the anger of God and of the judgment to come. In his distress, he tried to make reparation for some of the grossest of the wrongs which he had committed, but it was too late. After lingering a week or two in this condition of distress and suffering, his spirit passed away.

A.D. 1483

Effect of the tidings of Edward's death.

As the tidings of Edward's death spread throughout England, they were received every where with a sentiment of anxiety and suspense, for no one knew what the consequences would be. Edward left two sons. Edward, the oldest of the two, the Prince of Wales, was about thirteen years of age. The youngest, whose name was Richard, was eleven. Of course, Edward was the rightful heir to the crown. Next to him in the line of succession came his brother, and next to them came Richard, Duke of Gloucester, their uncle. But it was universally known that the Duke of Gloucester was a reckless and unscrupulous man, and the question in every one's mind was whether he would recognize the rights of his young nephews at all, or whether he would seize the crown at once for himself.

Richard, Duke of Gloucester, was in the northern part of England at this time, at the head of his army. The great power which the possession of this army gave him made people all the more fearful that he might attempt to usurp the throne.

Anxiety of Queen Elizabeth Woodville.

The person who was most anxious in respect to the result was the widowed Queen Elizabeth, the mother of the two princes. She was very much alarmed. The boys themselves were not old enough to realize very fully the danger that they were in, or to render their mother much aid in her attempts to save them. The person on whom she chiefly relied was her brother, the Earl of Rivers. Edward, her oldest son, was under this uncle Rivers's care. The uncle and the nephew were residing together at this time at the castle of Ludlow. Queen Elizabeth was in London with her second son.

Immediately on the death of the king, a council was called to deliberate upon the measures proper to be taken. The council decreed that the Prince of Wales should be proclaimed king, and they fixed upon the 4th of May for the day of his coronation. They also made arrangements for sending orders to the Earl of Rivers to come at once with the young king to London, in order that the coronation might take place.

Queen Elizabeth was present at this council, and she desired that her brother might be ordered to come attended by as large an armed force as he could raise, for the protection of the prince on the way.

Attempt made by Edward to effect a reconciliation.

Now it happened that there were great dissensions among the officers and nobles of the court at this time. The queen, with the relatives and connections of her family, formed one party, and the other nobles and peers of England another party, and great was the animosity and hatred that prevailed. The English nobles had never been satisfied with Edward's marriage, and they were very jealous of the influence of the queen's family and relations. This feud had been kept down in some degree while Edward lived, and Edward had made a great final effort to heal it entirely in his last sickness. He called together the leading nobles on each side, that had taken part in this quarrel, and then, by great exertion, went in among them, and urged them to forget their dissensions and become reconciled to each other. The effort for the time seemed to be successful, and both parties agreed to a compromise of the quarrel, and took a solemn oath that they would thenceforth live together in peace. But now, on the death of the king, the dissension broke out afresh. The other nobles were very jealous and suspicious of every measure which Elizabeth proposed, especially if it tended to continue the possession of power and influence in the hands of her family. Accordingly, when she proposed in the council to send for the earl, and to require him to raise a large escort to bring the young Prince Edward to London, they objected to it.

"Against whom," demanded one of the councilors, "is the young prince to be defended? Who are his enemies? He has none, and the real motive and design of raising this force is not to protect the prince, but only to secure to the Woodville family the means of increasing and perpetuating their own importance and power."

Plans for bringing the young prince to London.

The speaker upbraided the queen, too, with having, by this proposal, and by the attempt to promote the aggrandizement of the Woodville party which was concealed in it, been guilty of violating the oath of reconciliation which had been taken during the last sickness of the late king. So the council refused to authorize the armed escort, and the queen, with tears of disappointment and vexation, gave up the plan. At least she gave it up ostensibly, but she nevertheless contrived to come to some secret understanding with the earl, in consequence of which he set out from the castle with the young prince at the head of quite a large force. Some of the authorities state that he had with him two thousand men.

THE ATTEMPTED RECONCILIATION

Richard's movements.
His letter to the queen.

In the mean time, Richard of Gloucester, as soon as he heard of Edward's death, arranged his affairs at once, and made preparations to set out for London too. He put his army in mourning for the death of the king, and he wrote a most respectful and feeling letter of condolence to the queen. In this letter he made a solemn profession of homage and fealty to her son, the Prince of Wales, whom he acknowledged as rightfully entitled to the crown, and promised to be faithful in his allegiance to him, and to all the duties which he owed him.

Queen Elizabeth's mind was much relieved by this letter. She began to think that she was going to find in Richard an efficient friend to sustain her cause and that of her family against her enemies.

When Richard reached York, he made a solemn entry into that

town, attended by six hundred knights all dressed in deep mourning. At the head of this funeral procession he proceeded to the Cathedral, and there caused the obsequies of the king to be celebrated with great pomp, and with very impressive and apparently sincere exhibitions of the grief which he himself personally felt for the loss of his brother.

After a brief delay in York, Richard resumed his march to the southward. He arranged it so as to overtake the party of the prince and the Earl of Rivers on the way.

He arrives at Northampton.
The king at Stony Stratford.

He arrived at the town of Northampton on the same day that the prince, with the Earl of Rivers and his escort, reached the town of Stony Stratford, which was only a few miles from it. When the earl heard that Gloucester was so near, he took with him another nobleman, named Lord Gray, and a small body of attendants, and rode back to Northampton to pay his respects to Gloucester on the part of the young king; for they considered that Edward became at once, by the death of his father, King of England, under the style and title of Edward the Fifth.

Gloucester received his visitors in a very courteous and friendly manner. He invited them to sup with him, and he made quite an entertainment for them, and for some other friends whom he invited to join them. The party spent the evening together in a very agreeable manner.

Movements and manoeuvres at Northampton.

They sat so long over their wine that it was too late for the earl and Lord Gray to return that night to Stony Stratford, and Richard accordingly made arrangements for them to remain in Northampton. He assigned quarters to them in the town, and secretly set a guard over them, to prevent their making their escape. The next morning, when they arose, they were astonished to find themselves under guard, and to perceive too, as they did, that all the avenues of the town were occupied with troops. They suspected treachery, but they thought it not prudent to express their suspicions. Richard, when he met them again in the morning, treated them in the same friendly manner as on the evening before, and proposed to accompany them to Stony Stratford, in order that he might there see and pay his respects to the king. This was agreed to, and they all set out together.

In company with Richard was one of his friends and confederates, the Duke of Buckingham. This Duke of Buckingham had been one of the leaders of the party at court that were opposed to the family of the queen. These two, together with the Earl of Rivers and Lord Gray, rode on in a very friendly manner toward Stratford. They went in advance of Richard's troops, which were ordered to follow pretty closely behind. In this manner they went on till they began to draw near to the town.

Richard now at once threw off his disguise. He told the Earl of Rivers and Lord Gray that the influence which they were exerting over the mind of the king was evil, and that he felt it his duty to take the king from their charge.

The noblemen taken into custody.

Then, at a signal given, armed men came up and took the two noblemen in custody. Richard, with the Duke of Buckingham and their attendants, drove on with all speed into the town. It seems that the persons who had been left with Edward had, in some way or other, obtained intelligence of what was going on, for they were just upon the eve of making their escape with him when Richard and his party arrived. The horse was saddled, and the young king was all ready to mount.

Seizure of the king.

Richard, when he came up to the place, assumed the command at once. He made no obeisance to his nephew, nor did he in any other way seem to recognize or acknowledge him as his sovereign. He simply said that he would take care of his safety.

"The persons that have been about you," said he, "have been conspiring against your life, but I will protect you."

He then ordered several of the principal of Edward's attendants to be arrested; the rest he commanded to disperse. What became of the large body of men which the Earl of Rivers is said to have had under his command does not appear. Whether they dispersed in obedience to Richard's commands, or whether they abandoned the earl and came over to Richard's side, is uncertain. At any rate, nobody resisted him. The Earl of Rivers, Lord Gray, and the others were secured, with a view of being sent off prisoners to the northward. Edward himself was to be taken with Richard back to Northampton.

The little king is very much frightened.

The little king himself scarcely knew what to make of these proceedings. He was frightened; and when he saw that all those personal friends and attendants who had had the charge of him so long, and to whom he was strongly attached, were seized and sent away, and others, strangers to him, put in their place, he could not refrain from tears. King as he was, however, and sovereign ruler over millions of men, he was utterly helpless in his uncle's hands, and obliged to yield himself passively to the disposition which his uncle thought best to make of him.

All the accounts of Edward represent him as a kind-hearted and affectionate boy, of a gentle spirit, and of a fair and prepossessing countenance. The ancient portraits of him which remain confirm these accounts of his personal appearance and of his character.

ANCIENT PORTRAIT OF EDWARD V

Richard's explanations of his proceedings.

After having taken these necessary steps, and thus secured the power in his own hands, Richard vouchsafed an explanation of what he had done to the young king. He told him that Earl Rivers, and

Lord Gray, and other persons belonging to their party, "had conspired together to rule the kynge and the realme, to sette variance among the states, and to subdue and destroy the noble blood of the realme," and that he, Richard, had interposed to save Edward from their snares. He told him, moreover, that Lord Dorset, who was Edward's half brother, being the son of the queen by her first husband, and who had for some time held the office of Chancellor of the Tower, had taken out the king's treasure from that castle, and had sent much of it away beyond the sea.

Edward's astonishment.
He is helpless in Richard's hands.

Edward, astonished and bewildered, did not know at first what to reply to his uncle. He said, however, at last, that he never heard of any such designs on the part of his mother's relatives, and he could not believe that the charges were true. But Richard assured him that they were true, and that "his kindred had kepte their dealings from the knowledge of his grace." Satisfied or not, Edward was silenced; and he submitted, since it was hopeless for him to attempt to resist, to be taken back in his uncle's custody to Northampton.

Chapter XI
Taking Sanctuary

A.D. 1483

Alarm of the queen on hearing the news.

When the news reached London that the king had been seized on the way to the capital, and was in Gloucester's custody, it produced a universal commotion. Queen Elizabeth was thrown at once into a state of great anxiety and alarm. The tidings reached her at midnight. She was in the palace at Westminster at the time. She rose immediately in the greatest terror, and began to make preparations for fleeing to sanctuary with the Duke of York, her second son. All her friends in the neighborhood were aroused and summoned to her aid. The palace soon became a scene of universal confusion. Every body was busy packing up clothing and other necessaries in trunks and boxes, and securing jewels and valuables of various kinds, and removing them to places of safety. In the midst of this scene, the queen herself sat upon the rushes which covered the floor, half dressed, and her long and beautiful locks of hair streaming over her shoulders, the picture of despair.

Visit of the archbishop.
Hasting's message.

There was a certain nobleman, named Lord Hastings, who had been a very prominent and devoted friend to Edward the Fourth during his life, and had consequently been upon very intimate and friendly terms with the queen. It was he, however, that had objected in the council to the employment of a large force to conduct the young king to London, and, by so doing, had displeased the queen. Toward morning, while the queen was in the depths of her distress and terror, making her preparations for flight, a cheering message from Hastings was brought to her, telling her not to be alarmed. The message was brought to her by a certain archbishop who had been chancellor, that is, had had the custody of the great seal, an impression from which was necessary to the validity of any royal decree. He came to deliver up the seal to the queen, and also to bring Lord Hastings's message.

"Ah, woe worth him!" said the queen, when the archbishop informed her that Lord Hastings bid her not fear. "It is he that is the cause of all my sorrows; he goeth about to destroy me and my blood."

"Madam," said the archbishop, "be of good comfort. I assure you that, if they crown any other king than your eldest son, whom they have with them, we will, on the morrow, crown his brother, whom you have with you here. And here is the great seal, which, in like wise as your noble husband gave it to me, so I deliver it to you for the use of your son." So the archbishop delivered the great seal into the queen's hands, and went away. This was just before the dawn.

The queen is in great distress.

The words which the archbishop spoke to the queen did not give her much comfort. Indeed, her fears were not so much for her children, or for the right of the eldest to succeed to the throne, as for herself and her own personal and family ascendency under the reign of her son. She had contrived, during the lifetime of her husband, to keep pretty nearly all the influence and patronage of the government in her own hands and in that of her family connections, the Woodvilles. You will recollect how much difficulty that had made, and how strong a party had been formed against her coterie. And now, her husband being dead, what she feared was not that Gloucester, in taking the young king away from the custody of her relatives, and sending those relatives off as prisoners to the north, meant any hostility to the young king, but only against her and the whole Woodville interest, of which she was the head. She supposed that Gloucester would now put the power of the government in the hands of other families, and banish hers, and that perhaps he would even bring her to trial and punishment for acts of maladministration, or other political crimes which he would charge against her. It was fear of this, rather than any rebellion against the right of Edward the Fifth to reign, which made her in such haste to flee to sanctuary.

Uncertainty in respect to Gloucester's designs.

It was, however, somewhat uncertain what Gloucester intended to do. His professions were all very fair in respect to his allegiance to the young king. He sent a messenger to London, immediately after seizing the king, to explain his views and motives in the act, and in this communication he stated distinctly that his only object was to prevent the king's falling into the hands of the Woodville family, and not at all to oppose his coronation.

"It neyther is reason," said he in his letter, "nor in any wise to be suffered that the young kynge, our master and kinsman, should be in the hands of custody of his mother's kindred, sequestered in great measure from our companie and attendance, the which is neither honorable to hys majestie nor unto us."

Arrest of the leading men in the Woodville party.

Thus the pretense of Richard in seizing the king was simply that he might prevent the government under him from falling into the hands of his mother's party. But the very decisive measures he took in respect to the leading members of the Woodville family led many to suspect that he was secretly meditating a deeper design. All those who were with the king at the time of his seizure were made prisoners and sent off to a castle in the north, as we have already said; and, in order to prevent those who were in and near London from making their escape, Richard sent down immediately from Northampton ordering their arrest, and appointing guards to prevent any of them from flying to sanctuary. When the archbishop, who had called to see the queen at the palace, went away, he saw through the window, although it was yet before the dawn, a number of boats stationed on the Thames ready to intercept any who might be coming up the river with this intent from the Tower, for several influential members of the family resided at this time at the Tower.

The queen herself, however, as it happened, was at Westminster Palace, and she had accordingly but little way to go to make her escape to the Abbey.

The queen "on the rushes."
Her daughters.

The space which was inclosed by the consecrated limits, from within which prisoners could not be taken, was somewhat extensive. It included not only the church of the Abbey, but also the Abbey garden, the cemetery, the palace of the abbot, the cloisters, and various other buildings and grounds included within the inclosure. As soon as the queen entered these precincts, she sank down upon the floor of the hall, "alone on the rushes, all desolate and dismayed." It was in the month of May, and the great fire-place of the hall was filled with branches of trees and flowers, while the floor, according to the custom of the time, was strewed with green rushes. For a time the queen was so overwhelmed with her sorrow and chagrin that she was scarcely conscious where she was. But she was soon aroused from her despondency by the necessity of making proper arrangements for herself and her family in her new abode. She had two daughters with her, Elizabeth and Cecily—beautiful girls, seventeen and fifteen years of age; Richard, Duke of York, her second son, and several younger children. The youngest of these children, Bridget, was only three years old. Elizabeth, the oldest, afterward became a queen, and little Bridget a nun.

ANCIENT VIEW OF WESTMINSTER

Description of the sanctuary.
Apartments.

The rooms which the queen and her family occupied in the sanctuary are somewhat particularly described by one of the writers of those days. The fire-place, where the trees and flowers were placed, was in the centre of the hall, and there was an opening in the roof above, called a *louvre*, to allow of the escape of the smoke. This hearth still remains on the floor of the hall, and the louvre is still to be seen in the roof above. 7 The end of the hall was formed of oak panneling, with lattice-work above, the use of which will presently appear. A part of this paneling was formed of doors, which led by winding stairs up to a curious congeries of small rooms formed among the spaces between the walls and towers, and under the arches above. Some of these rooms were for private apartments, and others were used for the offices of buttery, kitchen, laundry, and the

---

7 The room is now the college hall, so called, of Westminster school.

like. At the end of this range of apartments was the private sitting-room and study of the abbot. The windows of the abbot's room looked down upon a pretty flower-garden, and there was a passage from it which led by a corridor back to the lattices over the doors in the hall, through which the abbot could look down into the hall at any time without being observed, and see what the monks were doing there.

The Jerusalem chamber.

Besides these there were other large apartments, called state apartments, which were used chiefly on great public occasions. These rooms were larger, loftier, and more richly decorated than the others. They were ornamented with oak carvings and fluting, painted windows, and other such decorations. There was one in particular, which was called the Jerusalem chamber. This was the grand receiving-room of the abbot. It had a great Gothic window of painted glass, and the walls were hung with curious tapestry. This room, with the window, the tapestry, and all the other ornaments, remains to this day.

Richard's plans in respect to the coronation.

It was on the night of the third of May that the queen and her family "took sanctuary." The very next day, the fourth, was the day that the council had appointed for the coronation. But Richard, instead of coming at once to London, after taking the king under his charge, so as to be ready for the coronation at the appointed day, delayed his journey so as not to enter London until that day. He wished to prevent the coronation from taking place, having probably other plans of his own in view instead.

Reception of Richard's party at London.

It is not, however, absolutely certain that Richard intended, at this time, to claim the crown for himself, for in entering London he formed a grand procession, giving the young king the place of honor in it, and doing homage to him as king. Richard himself and all his retinue were in mourning. Edward was dressed in a royal mantle of purple velvet, and rode conspicuously as the chief personage of the procession. A short distance from the city the cavalcade was met by a procession of the civic authorities of London and five hundred citizens, all sumptuously appareled, who had come out to receive and welcome their sovereign, and to conduct him through the gates into the city. In entering the city Richard rode immediately before the king, with his head uncovered. He held his cap in his hand, and bowed continually very low before the king, designating him in this way to the citizens as the object of their homage. He called out also, from time to time, to the crowds that thronged the waysides to see, "Behold your prince and sovereign."

Richard establishes his court.

There were two places to which it might have been considered not improbable that Richard would take the king on his arrival at the capital—one the palace of Westminster, at the upper end of London, and the other, the Tower, at the lower end. The Tower, though often used as a prison, was really, at that time, a castle, where the kings and the members of the royal family often resided. Richard, however, did not go to either of these places at first, but proceeded instead to the bishop's palace at St. Paul's, in the heart of the city. Here a sort of court was established, a grand council of nobles and officers of state was called, and for some days the laws were administered and the government was carried on from this place, all, however, in Edward's name. Money was coined, also, with his effigy and inscription, and, in fine, so far as all essential forms and technicalities were concerned, the young Edward was really a reigning king; but, of course, in respect to substantial power, every thing was in Richard's hands.

Dorset.

The reason why Richard did not proceed at once to the Tower was probably because Dorset, the queen's son, was in command there, and he, as of course he was identified with the Woodville party, might perhaps have made Richard some trouble. But Dorset, as soon as he heard that Richard was coming, abandoned the Tower, and fled to the sanctuary to join his mother. Accordingly, after waiting a few days at the bishop's palace until the proper arrangements could be made, the king, with the whole party in attendance upon him, removed to the Tower, and took up their residence there. The king was nominally in his castle, with Richard and the other nobles and their retinue in attendance upon him as his guards. Really he was in a prison, and his uncle, with the people around him who were under his uncle's command, were his keepers.

The queen's friends dismissed.
Richard's titles.

A meeting of the lords was convened, and various political

arrangements were made to suit Richard's views. The principal members of the Woodville family were dismissed from the offices which they held, and other nobles, who were in Richard's interest, were appointed in their place. A new day was appointed for the coronation, namely, the 22d of June. The council of lords decreed also that, as the king was yet too young to conduct the government himself personally, his uncle Gloucester was, for the present, to have charge of the administration of public affairs, under the title of Lord Protector. The title in full, which Richard thenceforth assumed under this decree, was, Richard, Duke of Gloucester, brother and uncle of the king, Protector and Defender, Great Chamberlain, Constable, and Lord High Admiral of England.

Anxiety of the people of England.

During all this time the city of London, and, indeed, the whole realm of England, as far as the tidings of what was going on at the capital spread into the interior, had been in a state of the greatest excitement. The nobles, and the courtiers of all ranks, were constantly on the alert, full of anxiety and solicitude, not knowing which side to take or what sentiments to avow. They did not know what turn things would finally take, and, of course, could not tell what they were to do in order to be found, in the end, on the side that was uppermost. The common people in the streets, with anxious looks and many fearful forebodings, discussed the reports and rumors that they had heard. They all felt a sentiment of loyal and affectionate regard for the king—a sentiment which was increased and strengthened by his youth, his gentle disposition, and the critical and helpless situation that he was in; while, on the other hand, the character of Gloucester inspired them with a species of awe which silenced and subdued them. Edward, in his "protector's" hands, seemed to them like a lamb in the custody of a tiger.

THE PEOPLE IN THE STREETS

Forlorn situation of the queen.

The queen, all this time, remained shut up in the sanctuary, in a state of extreme suspense and anxiety, clinging to the children whom she had with her, and especially to her youngest son, the little Duke of York, as the next heir to the crown, and her only stay and hope, in case, through Richard's violence or treachery, any calamity should befall the king.

Chapter XII
Richard Lord Protector

A.D. 1483

What sort of protection Richard afforded to the young wards who were committed to his charge will appear by events narrated in this chapter.

It was now June, and the day, the twenty-second, which had been fixed upon for the coronation, was drawing nigh. By the ancient usages of the realm of England, the office of Protector, to which Richard had been appointed, would expire on the coronation of the king. Of course, Richard perceived at once that if he wished to prolong his power he must act promptly.

Richard forms plans for seizing the crown.

He began to revolve in his mind the possibility of assuming the crown himself, and displacing the children of his older brothers; for Clarence left children at his decease as well as Edward. Of course, these children of Clarence, as well as those of Edward, would take precedence of him in the line of succession, being descended from an older brother. Richard therefore, in order to establish any claim to the crown for himself, must find some pretext for setting aside both these branches of the family. The pretexts which he found were these.

CLARENCE'S CHILDREN HEARING OF THEIR FATHER'S DEATH

His plan for disposing of Edward's children.

In respect to the children of Edward, his plan was to pretend to have discovered proof of Edward's having been privately married to another lady before his marriage with Elizabeth Woodville. This would, of course, render the marriage with Elizabeth Woodville null, and destroy the rights of the children to any inheritance from their father.

Clarence's children.

In respect to the children of Clarence, he was to maintain that they were cut off by the attainder which had been passed against their father. A bill of attainder, according to the laws and usages of those times, not only doomed the criminal himself to death, but cut off his children from all rights of inheritance. It was intended to destroy the family as well as the man.

Richard, however, did not at once reveal his plans, but proceeded cautiously to take the proper measures for putting them into execution.

Lady Cecily.
Baynard's Castle.

In the first place, there was his mother to be conciliated, the Lady Cecily Neville, known, however, more generally by the title of the Duchess of York. She lived at this time in an old family residence called Baynard's Castle, which stood on the banks of the Thames. As soon as Richard arrived in London he went to see his mother at this place, and afterward he often visited her there. How far he explained his plans to her, and how far she encouraged or disapproved of them, is not known. If she was required to act at all in the case, it must have been very hard for her, in such a question of life and death, to decide between her youngest son alive and the children of her first-born in his grave. Mothers can best judge to which side, in such an alternative, her maternal sympathies would naturally incline her.

Situation of the queen's friends at Pomfret Castle.

As for the immediate members of the Woodville family, they were already pretty well taken care of. The queen herself, with her children, were shut up in the sanctuary. Her brothers, and the other influential men who were most prominent on her side, had been made prisoners, and sent to Pomfret Castle in the north. Here they were held under the custody of men devoted to Richard's interest. But to prevent the possibility of his having any farther trouble with them, Richard resolved to order them to be beheaded. This resolution was soon carried into effect, as we shall presently see.

Lord Hastings.
Richard's councils.
The Tower.

There remained the party of nobles and courtiers that were likely to be hostile to the permanent continuance of the power of Richard, and inclined to espouse the cause of the young king. The nobles had not yet distinctly taken ground on this question. There were, however, some who were friendly to Richard. Others seemed more inclined to form a party against him. The prominent man among this last-named set was Lord Hastings. There were several others besides, and Richard knew very well who they were. In order to circumvent and defeat any plans which they might be disposed to form, and to keep the power fully in his own hands, he convened his councils of state at different places, sometimes at Westminster, sometimes at the Tower, where the king was kept, and sometimes at his own residence, which was in the heart of London. He transferred the public business more and more to his own residence, assembling the councilors there at all times, late and early, and thus withdrawing them from attendance at the Tower. Very soon Richard's residence in London became the acknowledged head-quarters of influence and power, and all who had petitions to present or favors to obtain gathered there, while the king in the Tower was neglected, and left comparatively alone.

Still the form of holding a council from time to time at the Tower was continued, and, of course, the nobles who assembled there were those most inclined to stand by and defend the cause of the king.

Such was the state of things on the 13th of June, nine days before the time appointed for the coronation. Richard then, having carefully laid his plans, was prepared to take decisive measures to break up the party who were disposed to gather around the king at the Tower and espouse his cause.

Nobles in council at the Tower.

On that day, while these nobles were holding a council in the Tower, suddenly, and greatly to their surprise, Richard walked in among them. He assumed a very good-natured and even merry air as he entered and took his seat, and began to talk with those present in a very friendly and familiar tone. This was for the purpose of lulling any suspicions which they might have felt on seeing him appear among them, and prevent them from divining the dreadful intentions with which he had come.

"My lord," said he, turning to a bishop who sat near him, and who was one of those that he was about to arrest, "you have some excellent strawberries in your garden, I understand. I wish you would let me have a plateful of them."

It was about the middle of June, you will recollect, which was the time for strawberries to be ripe.

The bishop was very much pleased to find the great Protector taking such an interest in his strawberries, and he immediately called a servant and sent him away at once to bring some of the fruit.

After having greeted the other nobles at the board in a somewhat similar style to this, with jocose and playful remarks, which had the effect of entirely diverting from their minds every thing like suspicion, he said that he must go away for a short time, but that he would presently return. In the mean time, they might proceed, he said, with their deliberations on the public business.

Richard's proceedings at the council.

So he went out. He proceeded at once to make the preparations necessary for the accomplishment of the desperate measures which he had determined to adopt. He stationed armed men at the doors and the passages of the part of the Tower where the council was assembled, and gave them instructions as to what they were to do, and agreed with them in respect to the signals which he was to give.

In about an hour he returned, but his whole air and manner were now totally changed. He came in with a frowning and angry countenance, knitting his brows and setting his teeth, as if something had occurred to put him in a great rage. He advanced to the council table, and there accosting Lord Hastings in a very excited and angry manner, he demanded,

"What punishment do you think men deserve who form plots and schemes for my destruction?"

Lord Hastings was amazed at this sudden appearance of displeasure, and he replied to the Protector that such men, if there were any such, most certainly deserved death, whoever they might be.

"It is that sorceress, my brother's wife," said Richard, "and that other vile sorceress, worse than she, Jane Shore. See!"

This allusion to Jane Shore was somewhat ominous for Hastings, as it was generally understood that since the king's death Lord Hastings had taken Jane Shore under his protection, and had lived in great intimacy with her.

As Richard said this, he pulled up the sleeve of his doublet to the elbow, to let the company look at his arm. This arm had always been weak, and smaller than the other.

"See," said he, "what they are doing to me."

He meant that by the power of necromancy they had made an image of wax as an effigy of him, according to the mode explained in a previous chapter, and were now melting it away by slow degrees in order to destroy his life, and that his arm was beginning to pine and wither away in consequence.

THE COUNCIL IN THE TOWER

Scene in the council chamber at the Tower.

The lords knew very well that the state in which they saw Richard's arm was its natural condition, and that, consequently, his charge against the queen and Jane Shore was only a pretense, which was to be the prelude and excuse for some violent measures that he was about to take. They scarcely knew what to say. At last Lord Hastings replied,

"Certainly, my lord, if they have committed so heinous an offense as this, they deserve a very heinous punishment."

"If!" repeated the Protector, in a voice of thunder. "And thou servest me, then, it seems, with *ifs* and *ands*. I tell thee that they *have* so done—and I will make what I say good upon thy body, traitor!"

He emphasized and confirmed this threat by bringing down his fist with a furious blow upon the table.

He makes signals for the armed men to come in.

This was one of the signals which he had agreed upon with the people that he had stationed without at the door of the council hall. A voice was immediately heard in the ante-chamber calling out Treason. This was again another signal. It was a call to a band of armed men whom Richard had stationed in a convenient place near by, and who were to rush in at this call. Accordingly, a sudden noise was heard of the rushing of men and the clanking of iron, and before the councilors could recover from their consternation the table was surrounded with soldiery, all "in harness," that is, completely armed, and as fast as the foremost came in and gathered around the table, others pressed in after them, until the room was completely full.

Richard, designating Hastings with a gesture, said suddenly, "I arrest thee, traitor."

"What! *me*, my lord?" exclaimed Hastings, in terror.

"Yes, thee, traitor."

Two or three of the soldiers immediately seized Hastings and prepared to lead him away. Other soldiers laid hands upon several of the other nobles, such as Richard had designated to them beforehand. These, of course, were the leading and prominent men of the party opposed to Richard's permanent ascendency. Most of these men were taken away and secured as prisoners in various parts of the Tower. As for Hastings, Richard, in a stern and angry manner, advised him to lose no time in saying his prayers, "for, by the Lord," said he, "I will not to dinner to-day till I see thy head off."

Hastings is executed.

Then, after a brief delay, to allow the wretched man a few minutes to say his prayers, Richard nodded to the soldiers to signify to them that they were to proceed to their work. They immediately took their victim out to a green by the side of the Tower, and, laying him down with his neck across a log which they found there, they cut off his head with a broad-axe.

POMFRET CASTLE

Orders sent to the north.

The same day Richard sent off a dispatch to the north, directed to the men who had in charge the Earl Rivers, and the other friends of the king who had been made prisoners when the king was seized at Stony Stratford, ordering them all to be beheaded. The order was immediately obeyed.

Execution of the prisoners at Pomfret Castle.

The person who had charge of the execution of this order was a stern and ruffian-like officer named Sir Richard Ratcliffe. This man is quite noted in the history of the times as one of the most unscrupulous of Richard's adherents. He was a merciless man, short and rude in speech, and reckless in action, destitute alike of all pity for man and of all fear of God.

The place where the prisoners had been confined was Pomfret Castle. On receiving the orders from Richard, Ratcliffe led them out to an open place without the castle wall to be beheaded. The executioners brought a log and an axe, and the victims were slaughtered one after another, without any ceremony, and without being allowed to say a word in self-defense.

The whole country was shocked at hearing of these sudden and terrible executions; but the power was in Richard's hands, and there was no one capable of resisting him. The death of the leaders of what would have been the young king's party struck terror into the rest, and Richard now had every thing in his own hands, or, rather, *almost* every thing; for the queen and her family, being still in the sanctuary, were beyond his reach. He, however, had nothing to fear from her personally, and there were none of the children that gave him any concern except the Duke of York, the king's younger brother. He, you will recollect, was with his mother at Westminster when the king was seized, and she had taken him with the other children to the Abbey. Richard was now extremely desirous of getting possession of this boy.

Richard's plans in respect to the Duke of York.
He determines to seize him.

The reason why he deemed it so essential to get possession of him was this. The child was, it is true, of little consequence while his brother the king lived; but if the king were put out of the way, then the thoughts and the hearts of all the loyal people of England, Richard knew very well, would be turned toward York as the rightful successor. But if they could both be put out of the way, and if the people of England could be induced to consider Clarence's children as set aside by the attainder of their father, then he himself would come forward as the true and rightful heir to the crown. It is true that it was a part of his plan, as has already been said, to declare the marriage of Elizabeth Woodville with the king null, and thus cut off both these children of Edward from their right of inheritance; but he knew very well that even if a majority of the people of England were to assent to this, there would certainly be a minority that would refuse their assent, and would adhere to the cause of the children, and they, if the children should fall into their hands, might, at some future time, make themselves very formidable to him, and threaten very seriously the permanence of his dominion. It was quite necessary, therefore, he thought, that he should get both children into his own power.

"I must," said he to himself, therefore, "I must, in some way or other, and at all hazards, get possession of little Richard."

The case of the little Richard argued.

It is always the policy of usurpers, and of all ambitious and aspiring men who wish to seize and hold power which does not properly belong to them, to carry the various measures necessary to the attainment of their ends, especially those likely to be unpopular, not by their own personal action, but by the agency of others, whom they put forward to act for them. Richard proceeded in this way in the present instance. He called a grand council of the peers of the realm and great officers of state, and caused the question to be brought up there of removing the young Duke of York from the custody of his mother to that of the Protector, in order that he might be with his brother. The peers who were in Richard's interest advocated this plan; but all the bishops and archbishops, who, of course, as ecclesiastics, had very high ideas of the sacredness and inviolability of a sanctuary, opposed the plan of taking the duke away except by the consent of his mother.

The other side argued in reply to them that a sanctuary was a place where persons could seek refuge to escape punishment in case of crime, and that where no crime could have been committed, and no charges of crime were made, the principle did not apply. In other words, that the sanctuary was for men and women who had been guilty, or were supposed to have been guilty, of violations of law; but as children could commit no crime for which an asylum was necessary, the privileges of sanctuary did not extend to them.

This view of the subject prevailed. The bishops and archbishops were outvoted, and an order in council was passed authorizing the Lord Protector to possess himself of his nephew, the Duke of York, and for this purpose to take him, if necessary, out of sanctuary by force.

Still, the bishops and archbishops were very unwilling that force should be used, if it could possibly be avoided; and finally the Archbishop of Canterbury, who was the highest prelate in the realm, proposed that a deputation from the council should be sent to the Abbey, and that he should go with them, in order to see the queen, and make the attempt to persuade her to give up her son of her own accord.

Delegation sent to the Tower.

After giving notice to the abbot of their intended visit, and making an arrangement with him and with the queen in respect to the time when they could be received, the delegation proceeded in state to the Abbey on the appointed day, and were received by the abbot and by Elizabeth with due ceremony in the Jerusalem chamber, the great audience hall of the Abbey, which has already been described.

Interview with the mother of the princes.

The Archbishop of Canterbury, who was at the head of the delegation, explained the case to the queen. They wished her, he said, to allow her son, the Duke of York, to leave the sanctuary, and to join his brother the king at his royal residence in the Tower. He would be perfectly safe there, he said, under the care of his uncle, the Lord Protector.

"The Protector thinks it very necessary that the duke should go," added the archbishop, "to be company for his brother. The king is very melancholy, he says, for want of a playfellow."

"And so the Protector," replied the queen—"God grant that he may really prove a protector—thinks that the king needs a playfellow! And can no playfellow be found for him except his brother?

"Besides," she added, "he is not in a mood to play. He is not well. They must find some other playmate for his brother. Just as if princes, while they are so young, could not as well have some one to play with them not of their own rank, or as if a boy must have his brother, and nobody else for his mate, when every body knows that boys are more likely to disagree with their brothers than they are with other children."

The archbishop, in reply, proceeded to argue the case with the queen, and to represent the necessity, arising from reasons of state, why the young duke should be committed to the charge of his uncle. He explained to her, too, that the Lord Protector had been fully authorized, by a decree of the council, to come and take his nephew from the Abbey, and to employ force, if necessary, to effect the purpose, but that it would be much better, both for the queen herself and the young duke, as well as for all concerned, that the affair should be settled in a peaceable and amicable manner.

The queen is forced to give up the child.

The unhappy queen saw at last that there was no alternative but for her to submit to her fate and give up her boy. Slowly and reluctantly she came to this conclusion, and finally gave her consent. Richard was brought in. His mother took him by the hand, and again addressed the archbishop and the delegation, speaking substantially as follows:

"My lord," said she, "and all my lords now present, I will not be so suspicious as to mistrust the promises you make me, or to believe that you are dealing otherwise than fairly and honorably by me. Here is my son. I give him up to your charge. I have no doubt that he would be safe here under my protection, if I could be allowed to keep him with me, although I have enemies that so hate me and all my blood, that I believe, if they thought they had any of it in their own veins, they would open them to let it flow out.

The parting scene.

"I give him up, at your demand, to the protection of his brother and his uncle. And yet I know well that the desire of a kingdom knows no kindred. Brothers have been their brothers' bane, and can these nephews be sure of their uncle? The boys would be safe if kept asunder; together—I do not know. Nevertheless, I here deliver my son, and with him his brother's life, into your hands, and of you shall I require them both, before God and man. I know that you are faithful and true in what you intend, and you have power, moreover, to keep the children safe, if you will. If you think that I am over-anxious and fear too much, take care that you yourselves do not fear too little."

Then drawing Richard to her, she kissed him very lovingly, the tears coming to her eyes as she did so.

"Farewell," she said, "farewell, mine own sweet son. God send you good keeping. I must kiss you before you go, for God knows when we shall kiss together again."

She kissed him again and blessed him, and then turned to go away, weeping bitterly.

The prince is taken away.

The child began to weep too, from sympathy with his mother's distress. The archbishop, however, took him by the hand and led him away, followed by the rest of the delegation.

They conveyed the young duke first to the hall of the council, which was very near, and thence to the Lord Protector's residence in the city. Here he was received with every mark of consideration and honor, and a handsome escort was provided to conduct him in state to the Tower, where he joined his brother.

Both princes entirely in Richard's power.

Richard had now every thing under his own control. The delivery of the Duke of York into his hands took place on the sixteenth of June. The time which had been set for the coronation was the twenty-second.

Chapter XIII
Proclaimed King

A.D. 1483

The Duke of Buckingham.
Historical doubts.
Richard, having thus obtained control of every thing essential to the success of his plans, began to prepare for action. His chief friend and confederate, the one on whom he relied most for the execution of the several measures which he proposed to take, was a powerful nobleman named the Duke of Buckingham. I shall proceed in this chapter to describe the successive steps of the course which Richard and the Duke of Buckingham pursued in raising Richard to the throne, as recorded by the different historians of those days, and as generally believed since, though, in fact, there have been great disputes in respect to these occurrences, and it is now quite difficult to ascertain with certainty what the precise truth of the case really is. This, however, is, after all, of no great practical importance, for, in respect to remote transactions of this nature, the thing which is most necessary for the purposes of general education is to understand what the story is, in detail, which has been generally received among mankind, and to which the allusions of orators and poets, and the discussions of statesmen and moralists in subsequent ages refer, for it is with this story alone that for all the purposes of general reading we have any thing to do.

Richard at Baynard's Castle.

Richard was residing at this time chiefly at Baynard's Castle with his mother. The young king and his brother, the Duke of York, were in the Tower. They were not nominally prisoners, but yet Richard kept close watch and ward over them, and took most effectual precautions to prevent their making their escape. The queen, Elizabeth Woodville, with her daughters, was in the sanctuary. Richard's wife, with the young child, was still at Middleham Castle.

The expense-book.
Items from the expense-book.

It is a very curious circumstance, showing how sometimes records of the most trivial and insignificant things come down to us from ancient times in a clear and certain form, while all that is really important to know is involved in doubt and obscurity—that the household expense-book of Anne at Middleham is still extant, showing all the little items of expense incurred for Richard's son, while all is dispute and uncertainty in respect to the great political schemes and measures of his father. In this book there is a charge of 22*s.* 9*d.* for a piece of green cloth, and another of 1*s.* 8*d.* for making it into gowns for "my lord prince." There is also a charge of 5*s.* for a feather for him, and 13*s.* 1*d.* paid to a shoemaker, named Dirick, for a pair of shoes. This expense-book was continued after Anne left Middleham Castle to go to London, as will be presently related. There are several charges on the journey for offerings and gifts made by the child at churches on the way. Two men were paid 6*s.* 8*d.* for running on foot by the side of his carriage. These men's names were Medcalf and Pacock. There is also a charge of 2*d.* for mending a whip!

Richard's plans.

But to return to our narrative. The time for the coronation of Edward the Fifth was drawing near, but Richard intended to prevent the performance of this ceremony, and to take the crown for himself instead. The first thing was to put in circulation the story that his two nephews were not the legitimate children of his brother, Edward the Fourth, and to prepare the way for this, he wished first, by every means, to cast odium on Edward's character. This was easily done, for Edward's character was bad enough to merit any degree of odium which his brother might wish it to bear.

Richard's determination in respect to Jane Shore.

Accordingly, Richard employed his friends and partisans in talking as much as possible in all quarters about the dissoluteness and the vices of the late king. False stories would probably have been invented, if it had not been that there were enough that were true. These stories were all revived and put in circulation, and every thing was made to appear as unfavorable for Edward as possible. Richard himself, on the other hand, feigned a very strict and scrupulous regard for virtue and morality, and deemed it his duty, he said, to do all in his power to atone for and wipe away the reproach which his brother's loose and wicked life had left upon the court and the kingdom. Among other things, the cause of public morals demanded, he said, that an example should be made of Jane Shore, who had been the associate and partner of the king in his immoralities.

Jane's character.

Jane Shore, it will be recollected, was the wife of a rich citizen of London, whom Edward had enticed away from her husband and brought to court. She was naturally a very amiable and kind-hearted woman, and all accounts concur in saying that she exercised the power that she acquired over the mind of the king in a very humane and praiseworthy manner. She was always ready to interpose, when the king contemplated any act of harshness or severity, to avert his anger and save his intended victim, and, in general, she did a great deal to soften the brutality of his character, and to protect the innocent and helpless from the wrongs which he would otherwise have often done them. These amiable and gentle traits of character do not, indeed, atone at all for the grievous sin which she committed in abandoning her husband and living voluntarily with the king, but they did much toward modifying the feeling of scorn and contempt with which she would have otherwise been regarded by the people of England.

Her jewelry confiscated.
The punishment of Jane Shore.

Richard caused Jane to be arrested and sent to prison. He also seized all her plate and jewels, and confiscated them. She had a very rich and valuable collection of these things. [8] Richard then caused an ecclesiastical court to be organized, and sent her before it to be tried. The court, undoubtedly in accordance with instructions that Richard himself gave them, sentenced her, by way of penance for her sins, to walk in midday through the streets of London, from one end of the city to the other, almost entirely undressed. The intention of this severe exposure was to designate her to those who should assemble to witness the punishment as a wanton, and thus to put her to shame, and draw upon her the scorn and derision of the populace. They found some old and obsolete law which authorized such a punishment. The sentence was carried into effect on a Sunday. The unhappy criminal was conducted through the principal streets of the city, wearing a night-dress, and carrying a lighted taper in her hand, between rows of spectators that assembled by

---

[8] The husband with whom she had lived before she became acquainted with Edward was a wealthy goldsmith and jeweler.

thousands along the way to witness the scene. But, instead of being disposed to receive her with taunts and reproaches, the populace were moved to compassion by her saddened look and her extreme beauty. Their hearts were softened by the remembrance of the many stories they had heard of the kindness of her heart, and the amiableness and gentleness of her demeanor, in the time of her prosperity and power. They thought it hard, too, that the law should be enforced so rigidly against her alone, while so many multitudes in all ranks of society, high as well as low, were allowed to go unpunished.

Still, Richard's object in this exhibition was accomplished. The transaction had the effect of calling the attention of the public universally and strongly to the fact that Edward the Fourth had been a loose and dissolute man, and prepared people's minds for the charge which was about to be brought against him.

Alleged marriage of Edward IV. to Elinor Talbot.

This charge was that he had been secretly married to another lady before his union with Elizabeth Woodville, and that consequently by this latter marriage he was guilty of bigamy. Of course, if this were true, the second marriage would be null and void, and the children springing from it would have no rights as heirs.

Particulars of the story.

Whether there was any truth in this story or not can not now ever be certainly known. All that is certain is that Richard circulated the report, and he found several witnesses to testify to the truth of it. The maiden name of the lady to whom they said the king had been married was Elinor Talbot. She had married in early life a certain Lord Boteler, whose widow she was at the time that Edward was alleged to have married her. The marriage was performed in a very private manner by a certain bishop, nobody being present besides the parties except the bishop himself, and he was strictly charged by the king to keep the affair a profound secret. This he promised to do. Notwithstanding his promise, however, the bishop some time subsequently, after the king had been married to Elizabeth Woodville, revealed the secret of the previous marriage to Gloucester, at which the king, when he heard of it, was extremely angry. He accused the bishop of having betrayed the trust which he had reposed in him, and, dismissing him at once from office, shut him up in prison.

Richard having, as he said, kept these facts secret during his brother's lifetime, out of regard for the peace of the family, now felt it his duty to make them known, in order to prevent the wrong which would be done by allowing the crown to descend to a son who, not being born in lawful wedlock, could have no rights as heir.

After disseminating this story among the influential persons connected with the court, and through all the circles of high life, during the week, it was arranged that on the following Sunday the facts should be made known publicly to the people.

Plan for publishing it.

There was a large open space near St. Paul's Cathedral, in the very heart of London, where it was the custom to hold public assemblies of all kinds, both religious and political. There was a pulpit built on one side of this space, from which sermons were preached, orations and harangues pronounced, and proclamations made. Oaths were administered here too, in cases where it was required to administer oaths to large numbers of people.

Sermon preached by Dr. Shaw near St. Paul's.

From this pulpit, on the next Sunday after the penance of Jane Shore, a certain Dr. Shaw, who was a brother of the Lord-mayor of London, preached a sermon to a large concourse of citizens, in which he openly attempted to set aside the claims of the two boys, and to prove that Richard was the true heir to the crown.

He took for his text a passage from the Wisdom of Solomon, "The multiplying brood of the ungodly shall not thrive." In this discourse he explained to his audience that Edward, when he was married to Elizabeth Woodville, was already the husband of Elinor Boteler, and consequently that the second marriage was illegal and void, and the children of it entirely destitute of all claims to the crown. He also, it is said, advanced the idea that neither Edward nor Clarence were the children of their reputed father, the old Duke of York, but that Richard was the oldest legitimate son of the marriage, in proof of which he offered the fact that Richard strongly resembled the duke in person, while neither Edward nor Clarence had borne any resemblance to him at all.

Ingenious contrivance.
Coolness of the people.

It was arranged, moreover—so it was said—that, when the preacher came to the passage where he was to speak of the resemblance which Richard bore to his father, the great Duke of York, Richard himself was to enter the assembly as if by accident, and thus give the preacher the opportunity to illustrate and confirm what he had said by directing his audience to observe for themselves the resemblance which he had pointed out, and also to excite them to a burst of enthusiasm in Richard's favor by the eloquent appeal which the incident of Richard's entrance was to awaken. But this intended piece of stage effect, if it was really planned, failed in the execution. Richard did not come in at the right time, and when he did come in, either the preacher managed the case badly, or else the people were very little disposed to espouse Richard's cause; for when the orator, at the close of his appeal, expected applause and acclamations, the people uttered no response, but looked at each other in silence, and remained wholly unmoved.

Meeting at the Guildhall.

In the course of the following two or three days, other attempts were made to excite the populace to some demonstration in Richard's favor, but they did not succeed. The Duke of Buckingham met a large concourse of Londoners at the Guildhall, which is in the centre of the business portion of the city. He was supported by a number of nobles, knights, and distinguished citizens, and he made a long and able speech to the assembly, in which he argued strenuously in favor of calling Richard to the throne. He denounced the character of the former king, and enlarged at length on the dissipated and vicious life which he had led. He also related to the people the story of Edward's having been the husband of Lady Elinor Boteler at the time when his marriage with Queen Elizabeth took place, which fact, as Buckingham showed, made the marriage with Elizabeth void, and cut off the children from the inheritance. The children of Clarence had been cut off, too, by the attainder, and so Richard was the only remaining heir.

The people do not respond.

The duke concluded his harangue by asking the assembly if, under those circumstances, they would not call upon Richard to ascend the throne. A few of the poorer sort, very likely some that had been previously hired to do it, threw up their caps into the air in response to this appeal, and cried out, "Long live King Richard!" But the major part, comprising all the more respectable portion of the assembly, looked grave and were silent. Some who were pressed to give their opinion said they must take time to consider.

The appeals to the people fail.

Thus these appeals to the people failed, so far as the object of them was to call forth a popular demonstration in Richard's favor. But in one respect they accomplished the object in view: they had the effect of making it known throughout London and the vicinity that a revolution was impending, and thus preparing men's minds to acquiesce in the change more readily than they might perhaps have done if it had come upon them suddenly and with a shock.

Grand council convened.
Arrangements made by Buckingham.

On the following day after the address at the Guildhall, a grand assembly of all the lords, bishops, councilors, and officers of state was convened in Westminster. It was substantially a Parliament, though not a Parliament in form. The reason why it was not called as a Parliament in form was because Richard, having doubts, as he said, about the right of Edward to the throne, could not conscientiously advise that any public act should be performed in his name, and a Parliament could only be legally convened by summons from a king. Accordingly, this assembly was only an informal meeting of the peers of England and other great dignitaries of Church and State, with a view of consulting together to determine what should be done. Of course, it was all fully arranged and settled beforehand, among those who were in Richard's confidence, what the result of these deliberations was to be. The Duke of Buckingham, Richard's principal friend and supporter, managed the business at the meeting. The assembly consisted, of course, chiefly of the party of Richard's friends. The principal leaders of the parties opposed to him had been beheaded or shut up in prison; of the rest, some had fled, some had concealed themselves, and of the few who dared to show themselves at the meeting, there were none who had the courage, or perhaps I ought rather to say the imprudence and folly, to oppose any thing which Buckingham should undertake to do.

The petition.

The result of the deliberations of this council was the drawing up of a petition to be presented to Richard, declaring him the true and rightful heir to the crown, and praying him to assume at once the sovereign power.

Substance of the petition.

A delegation was appointed to wait upon Richard and present the petition to him. Buckingham was at the head of this delegation. The petition was written out in due form upon a roll of parchment. It declared that, inasmuch as it was clearly established that King Edward the Fourth was already the husband of "Dame Alionora Boteler," by a previous marriage, at the time of his pretended marriage with Elizabeth Woodville, and that consequently his children by Elizabeth Woodville, not being born in lawful wedlock, could have no rights of inheritance whatever from their father, and especially could by no means derive from him any title to the crown; and inasmuch as the children of Clarence had been cut off from the succession by the bill of attainder which had been passed against their father; and inasmuch as Richard came next in order to these in the line of succession, therefore he was now the true and rightful heir. This his right moreover by birth was now confirmed by the decision of the estates of the realm assembled for the purpose; wherefore the petition, in conclusion, invited and urged him at once to assume the crown which was thus his by a double title—the right of birth and the election of the three estates of the realm.

Real object of it.

Of course, although the petition was addressed to Richard as if the object of it was to produce an effect upon his mind, it was really all planned and arranged by Richard himself, and by Buckingham in conjunction with him; and the representations and arguments which it contained were designed solely for effect on the mind of the public, when the details of the transaction should be promulgated throughout the land.

The petition being ready, Buckingham, in behalf of the delegation, demanded an audience of the Lord Protector that they might lay it before him. Richard accordingly made an appointment to receive them at his mother's residence at Baynard's Castle.

Richard receives the petition at Baynard's Castle.

At the appointed time the delegation appeared, and were received in great state by Richard in the audience hall. The Duke of Buckingham presented the petition, and Richard read it. He seemed surprised, and he pretended to be at a loss what to reply. Presently he began to say that he could not think of assuming the crown. He said he had no ambition to reign, but only desired to preserve the kingdom for his nephew the king until he should become of sufficient age, and then to put him peaceably in possession of it. But the Duke of Buckingham replied that this could never be. The people of England, he said, would never consent to be ruled by a prince of illegitimate birth.

"And if you, my lord," added the duke, "refuse to accept the crown, they know where to find another who will gladly accept it."

BAYNARD'S CASTLE

Richard concludes to accept the crown.

In the end, Richard allowed himself to be persuaded that there was no alternative but for him to accept the crown, and he reluctantly consented that, on the morrow, he would proceed in state to Westminster, and publicly assume the title and the prerogatives of king.

Accordingly, the next day, a grand procession was formed, and Richard was conducted with great pomp to Westminster Hall. Here he took his place on the throne, with the leading lords of his future court, and the bishops and archbishops around him. The rest of the hall was crowded with a vast concourse of people that had assembled to witness the ceremony.

First the king took the customary royal oath, which was administered by the archbishop. He then summoned the great judges before him, and made an address to them, exhorting them to administer the laws and execute judgment between man and man in a just and impartial manner, inasmuch as to secure that end, he said, would be the first and greatest object of his reign.

After this Richard addressed the concourse of people in the hall, who, in some sense, represented the public, and pronounced a pardon for all offenses which had been committed against himself, and ordered a proclamation to be made of a general amnesty throughout the land. These announcements were received by the people with loud acclamations, and the ceremony was concluded by shouts of "Long live King Richard!" from all the assembly.

We obtain a good idea of this scene by the following engraving, which is copied exactly from a picture contained in a manuscript volume of the time.

THE KING ON HIS THRONE

Ceremonies connected with the investiture of the king.

The royal dignity having thus been assumed by the new king at the usual centre and seat of the royal power, the procession was again formed, and Richard was conducted to Westminster Abbey for the purpose of doing the homage customary on such occasions at one of the shrines in the church. The procession of the king was met at the door of the church by a procession of monks chanting a solemn anthem as they came.

Richard marches through London.
Is every where proclaimed king.

After the religious ceremonies were completed, Richard, at the head of a grand cavalcade of knights, noblemen, and citizens, proceeded into the city to the Church of St. Paul. The streets were lined with spectators, who saluted the king with cheers and acclamations as he passed. At the Church of St. Paul more ceremonies were performed and more proclamations were made. The popular joy, more or less sincere, was expressed by the sounding of trumpets, the waving of banners, and loud acclamations of "Long live King Richard!" At length, when the services in the city were concluded, the king returned to Westminster, and took up his abode at the royal palace; and while he was returning, heralds were sent to all the great centres of concourse and intelligence in and around London to proclaim him king.

Extraordinary character of the reign of Edward V.

This proclamation of Richard as king took place on the twenty-sixth of June. King Edward the Fourth died just about three months before. During this three months Edward the Fifth is, in theory, considered as having been the King of England, though, during the whole period, the poor child, instead of exercising any kingly rights or prerogatives, was a helpless prisoner in the hands of others, who, while they professed to be his protectors, were really his determined and relentless foes.

Chapter XIV
The Coronation

A.D. 1483

Plan for the coronation.

It was on the 26th of June, 1483, that Richard was proclaimed king, under the circumstances narrated in the last chapter. In order to render his investiture with the royal authority complete, he resolved that the ceremony of coronation should be immediately performed. He accordingly appointed the 6th of July for the day. This allowed an interval of just ten days for the necessary preparations.

Anne is sent for, and comes to London.

The first thing to be done was to send to Middleham Castle for Anne, his wife, who now, since the proclamation of Richard, became Queen of England. Richard wished that she should be present, and take part in the ceremony of the coronation. The child was to be brought too. His name was Edward.

It seems that Anne arrived in London only on the 3d of July, three days before the appointed day. There is a specification in the book of accounts of some very elegant and costly cloth of gold bought on that day in London, the material for the queen's coronation robe.

Richard determined that the ceremony of his coronation should be more magnificent than that of any previous English monarch. Preparations were made, accordingly, on a very grand scale. There were several preliminary pageants and processions on the days preceding that of the grand ceremony.

Procession of barges.

On the 4th of July, which was Sunday, the king and queen proceeded in state to the Tower. They went in barges on the river. The party set out from Baynard's Castle, the residence of Richard's mother, and the place where the queen went on her arrival in London.

Great crowds of spectators.
The royal barges.

The royal barges destined to convey the king and queen, and the other great personages of the party, were covered with canopies of silk and were otherwise magnificently adorned. Great crowds of spectators assembled to witness the scene. Some came in boats upon the water, others took their stations on the shores, where every prominent and commanding point was covered with its own special crowd, and others still occupied the windows of the buildings that looked out upon the river.

Through the midst of this scene the royal barges passed down the river to the Tower. As they moved along, the air was filled with prolonged and continual shouts of "Long live King Richard!" "Long live the noble Queen Anne!"

Royal or imperial power, once firmly established, will never fail to draw forth the acclamations of the crowd, no matter by what means it has been acquired.

Arrival at the Tower.
Measures adopted.

On his arrival at the Tower, Richard was received with great honor by the authorities which he had left in charge there, and he took possession of the edifice formally, as one of his own royal residences. He held a court in the great council-hall. At this court he created several persons peers of the realm, and invested others with the honor of knighthood. These were men whom he supposed to be somewhat undecided in respect to the course which they should pursue, and he wished, by these compliments and honors, to purchase their adhesion to his cause.

He also liberated some persons who had been made prisoners, presuming that, by this kindness, he should conciliate their good-will.

The princes imprisoned.

He did not, however, by any means extend this conciliating policy to the case of the young ex-king and his brother; indeed, it would have been extremely dangerous for him to have done so. He was aware that there must be a large number of persons throughout the kingdom who still considered Edward as the rightful king, and he knew very well that, if any of these were to obtain possession of Edward's person, it would enable them to act vigorously in his name, and to organize perhaps a powerful party for the support of his claims. He was convinced, therefore, that it was essential to the success of his plans that the boys should be kept in very close and safe custody. So he removed them from the apartments which they had hitherto occupied, and shut them up in close confinement in a gloomy tower upon the outer walls of the fortress, and which, on account of the cruel murders which were from time to time committed there, subsequently acquired the name of the Bloody Tower.

THE BLOODY TOWER

Richard and Anne proceed to Westminster.

Richard and the queen remained at the Tower until the day appointed for the coronation, which was Tuesday. The ceremonies of that day were commenced by a grand progress of the king and his suite through the city of London back to Westminster, only, as if to vary the pageantry, they went back in grand cavalcade through the streets of the city, instead of returning as they came, by barges on the river. The concourse of spectators on this occasion was even greater than before. The streets were every where thronged, and very strict regulations were made, by Richard's command, to prevent disorder.

Ceremonies connected with the coronation.

On arriving at Westminster, the royal party proceeded to the Abbey, where, first of all, as was usual in the case of a coronation, certain ceremonies of religious homage were to be performed at a particular shrine, which was regarded as an object of special sanctity on such occasions. The king and queen proceeded to this shrine from the great hall, barefooted, in token of reverence and humility. They walked, however, it should be added, on ornamented cloth laid down for this purpose on the stone pavements of the floors. All the knights and nobles of England that were present accompanied and followed the king and queen in their pilgrimage to the shrine.

The royal paraphernalia.

One of these nobles bore the king's crown, another the queen's crown, and others still various other ancient national emblems of royal power. The queen walked under a canopy of silk, with a golden bell hanging from each of the corners of it. The canopy was borne by four great officers of state, and the bells, of course, jingled as the bearers walked along.

The queen wore upon her head a circlet of gold adorned with precious stones. There were four bishops, one at each of the four corners of the canopy, who walked as immediate attendants upon the queen, and a lady of the very highest rank followed her, bearing her train.

Religious services.

When the procession reached the shrine, the king and queen took their seats on each side of the high altar, and then there came forth a procession of priests and bishops, clothed in magnificent sacerdotal robes made of cloth of gold, and chanting solemn hymns of prayer and praise as they came.

The king and queen crowned.

After the religious services were completed, the ceremony of anointing and crowning the king and queen, and of investing their persons with the royal robes and emblems, was performed with the usual grand and imposing solemnities. After this, the royal cortége was formed again, and the company returned to Westminster Hall in the same order as they came. The queen walked, as before, under her silken canopy, the golden bells keeping time, by their tinkling, with the steps of the bearers.

The dais.

At Westminster Hall a great dais had been erected, with thrones upon it for the king and queen. As their majesties advanced and ascended this dais, surrounded by the higher nobles and chief officers of state, the remainder of the procession, consisting of those who had come to accompany and escort them to the place, followed, and filled the hall.

Ceremonial in Westminster Hall.

As soon as this vast throng saw that the king and queen were seated upon the dais, with their special and immediate attendants around them, their duties were ended, and they were to be dismissed. A grand officer of state, whose duty it was to dismiss them, came in on horseback, his horse covered with cloth of gold hanging down on both sides to the ground. The people, falling back before this horseman, gradually retired, and thus the hall was cleared.

The king and queen then rose from their seats upon the dais, and were conducted to their private apartments in the palace, to rest and refresh themselves after the fatigues of the public ceremony, and to prepare for the grand banquet which was to take place in the evening.

The preparations for this banquet were made by spreading a table upon the dais under the canopy for the king and queen, and four other very large and long tables through the hall for the invited guests.

The banquet.

The time appointed for the banquet was four o'clock. When the hour arrived, the king and queen were conducted into the hall again, and took their places at the table which had been prepared for them on the dais. They had changed their dresses, having laid aside their royal robes, and the various paraphernalia of office with which they had been indued at the coronation, and now appeared in robes of crimson velvet embroidered with gold, and trimmed with costly furs. They were attended by many lords and ladies of the highest rank, scarcely less magnificently dressed than themselves. They were waited upon, while at table, by the noblest persons in the realm, who served them from the most richly wrought vessels of gold and silver.

The royal champion.

After the first part of the banquet was over, a knight, fully armed, and mounted on a warhorse richly caparisoned, rode into the hall, having been previously announced by a herald. This was the king's champion, who came, according to a custom usually observed on such occasions, to challenge and defy the king's enemies, if any such there were.

Grand challenge.

The trappings of the champion's horse were of white and red silk, and the armor of the knight himself was bright and glittering. As he rode forward into the area in front of the dais, he called out, in a loud voice, demanding of all present if there were any one there who disputed the claim of King Richard the Third to the crown of England.

All the people gazed earnestly at the champion while he made this demand, but no one responded.

Gauntlet thrown down.

The champion then made proclamation again, that if any one there was who would come forward and say that King Richard was not lawfully King of England, he was ready there to fight him to the death, in vindication of Richard's right. As he said this, he threw down his gauntlet upon the floor, in token of defiance.

The spectators.

At this, the whole assembly, with one voice, began to shout, "Long live King Richard!" and the immense hall was filled, for some minutes, with thundering acclamations.

A largesse.

This ceremony being concluded, a company of heralds came forward before the king, and proclaimed "a largesse," as it was called. The ceremony of a largesse consisted in throwing money among the crowd to be scrambled for. Three times the money was thrown out, on this occasion, among the guests in the hall. The amount that is charged on the royal account-book for the expense of this largesse is one hundred pounds.

Modern largesses.

The scrambling of a crowd for money thrown thus among them, one would say, was a very rude and boisterous amusement, but those were rude and boisterous times. The custom holds its ground in England, in some measure, to the present day, though now it is confined to throwing out pence and halfpence to the rabble in the streets at an election, and is no longer, as of yore, relied upon as a means of entertaining noble guests at a royal dinner.

The torches.

After the frolic of the largesse was over, the king and queen rose to depart. The evening was now coming on, and a great number of torches were brought in to illuminate the hall. By the light of these torches, the company, after their majesties had retired, gradually withdrew, and the ceremonies of the coronation were ended.

The king resolves on a grand progress through the kingdom.

After the coronation, King Richard and Anne, the queen, went to Windsor, and took up their residence there, with the court, for a short time, in order that Richard might attend to the most important of the preliminary arrangements for the management of public affairs, which are always necessary at the commencement of a new reign. As soon as these things were settled, the king set out to make a grand progress through his dominions, for the purpose of receiving the congratulations of the people, and also of impressing them, as much as possible, with a sense of his grandeur and power by the magnificence of his retinue, and the great parades and celebrations by which his progress through the country was to be accompanied.

Oxford.
State of public sentiment.

From Windsor Castle the king went first to Oxford, where he was received with distinguished honors by all the great dignitaries connected with the University. Hence he proceeded to Gloucester, and afterward to Worcester. At all these places he was received with great parade and pageantry. Those who were disposed to espouse his cause, of course, endeavored to gain his favor by doing all in their power to give éclat to these celebrations. Those who were indifferent or in doubt, flocked, of course, to see the shows, and thus involuntarily contributed to the apparent popularity of the demonstrations; while, on the other hand, those who were opposed to him, and adhered still secretly to the cause of young King Edward, made no open opposition, but expressed their dissent, if they expressed it at all, in private conclaves of their own. They could not do otherwise than to allow Richard to have his own way during the hour of his triumph, *their* hour being not yet come.

Warwick Castle.

At last, Richard, in his progress, reached Warwick Castle, and here he was joined by the queen and the young prince, who had remained at Windsor while the king was making his tour through the western towns, but who now came across the country with a grand retinue of her own, to join her husband at her own former home; for Warwick Castle was the chief stronghold and principal residence of the great Earl of Warwick, the queen's father. The king and queen remained for some time at Warwick Castle, and the king established his court here, and maintained it with great pomp and splendor. Here he received embassadors from Spain, France, and Burgundy, who had been sent by their several governments to congratulate him on his accession, and to pay him their homage. Each of these embassadors came in great state, and were accompanied by a grand retinue; and the ceremonies of receiving them, and the entertainments given to do them honor, were magnificent beyond description.

Embassadors.

One of these embassadors, the one sent by the government of Spain, brought a formal proposal from Ferdinand and Isabella for a marriage between their daughter and Richard's little son. The little prince was at that time about seven years of age.

Arrival at York.

After remaining some time at Warwick Castle, the royal party proceeded northward, and, after passing through several large towns, they arrived finally at York, which was then, in some sense, the northern capital of the kingdom. Here there was another grand reception. All the nobility and gentry of the surrounding country came in to honor the king's arrival, and the ceremonies attending the entrance of the royal cortége were extremely magnificent.

The coronation repeated.
Richard's son.

While the court was at York, Richard repeated the ceremony of the coronation. On this occasion, his son, the little Prince Edward, was brought forward in a conspicuous manner. He was created Prince of Wales with great ceremony, and on the day of the coronation he had a little crown upon his head, and his mother led him by the hand in the procession to the altar.

The poor child did not live, however, to realize the grand destiny which his father thus marked out for him. He died a few months after this at Middleham Castle.

Celebrations and rejoicings.

The coronation at York was attended and followed, as that at London had been, with banquets and public parades, and grand celebrations of all sorts, which continued for several successive days, and the hilarity and joy which these shows awakened among the crowds that assembled to witness them seemed to indicate a universal acquiescence on the part of the people of England in Richard's accession to the throne.

Still, although outwardly every thing looked fair, Richard's mind was not yet by any means at ease. From the very day of his accession, he knew well that, so long as the children of his brother Edward remained alive at the Tower, his seat on the throne could not be secure. There must necessarily be, he was well aware, a large party in the kingdom who were secretly in favor of Edward, and he knew that they would very soon begin to come to an understanding with each other, and to form plans for effecting a counter-revolution. The most certain means of preventing the formation of these plots, or of defeating them, if formed, would be to remove the children out of the way. He accordingly determined in his heart, before he left London, that this should be done.[9]

His determination in respect to the children.

He resolved to put them to death. The deed was to be performed during the course of his royal progress to the north, while the minds of the people of England were engrossed with the splendor of the pageantry with which his progress was accompanied. He intended, moreover, that the murder should be effected in a very secret manner, and that the death of the boys should be closely concealed until a time and occasion should arrive rendering it necessary that it should be made public.

His agent Green.

Accordingly, soon after he left London, he sent back a confidential agent, named Green, to Sir Robert Brakenbury, the governor of the Tower, with a letter, in which Sir Robert was commanded to put the boys to death.

---

[9] I say he determined; for, although some of Richard's defenders have denied that he was guilty of the crime which the almost unanimous voice of history charges upon him, the evidence leaves very little room to doubt that the dreadful tale is in all essential particulars entirely true.

Green's return.

Green immediately repaired to London to execute the commission. Richard proceeded on his journey. When he arrived at Warwick, Green returned and joined him there, bringing back the report that Sir Robert refused to obey the order.

Conversation with the page.

Richard was very angry when Green delivered this message. He turned to a page who was in waiting upon him in his chamber, and said, in a rage,

"Even these men that I have brought up and made, refuse to obey my commands."

The page replied,

"Please your majesty, there is a man here in the ante-chamber, that I know, who will obey your majesty's commands, whatever they may be."

Sir James Tyrrel.

Richard asked the page who it was that he meant, and he said Sir James Tyrrel. Sir James Tyrrel was a very talented and accomplished, but very unscrupulous man, and he was quite anxious to acquire the favor of the king. The page knew this, from conversation which Sir James had had with him, and he had been watching an opportunity to recommend Sir James to Richard's notice, according to an arrangement that Sir James had made with him.

Richard employs Tyrrel.
The letter.

So Richard ordered that Sir James should be sent in. When he came, Richard held a private conference with him, in which he communicated to him, by means of dark hints and insinuations, what he required. Tyrrel undertook to execute the deed. So Richard gave him a letter to Sir Robert Brakenbury, in which he ordered Sir Robert to deliver up the keys of the Tower to Sir James, "to the end," as the letter expressed it, "that he might there accomplish the king's pleasure in such a thing as he had given him commandment."

Sir James, having received this letter, proceeded to London, taking with him such persons as he thought he might require to aid him in his work. Among these was a man named John Dighton. John Dighton was Sir James's groom. He was "a big, broad, square, strong knave," and ready to commit any crime or deed of violence which his master might require.

Tyrrel arrives at the Tower.

On arriving at the Tower, Sir James delivered his letter to the governor, and the governor gave him up the keys. Sir James went to see the keepers of the prison in which the boys were confined. There were four of them. He selected from among these four, one, a man named Miles Forest, whom he concluded to employ, together with his groom, John Dighton, to kill the princes. He formed the plan, gave the men their instructions, and arranged it with them that they were to carry the deed into execution that night.

Murder of the princes.
Action of the assassins.

Accordingly, at midnight, when the princes were asleep, the two men stole softly into the room, and there wrapped the poor boys up suddenly in the bed-clothes, with pillows pressed down hard over their faces, so that they could not breathe. The boys, of course, were suddenly awakened, in terror, and struggled to get free; but the men held them down, and kept the pillows and bed-clothes pressed so closely over their faces that they could not breathe or utter any cry. They held them in this way until they were entirely suffocated.

When they found that their struggles had ceased, they slowly opened the bed-clothes and lifted up the pillows to see if their victims were really dead.

"Yes," said they to each other, "they are dead."

The murderers took off the clothes which the princes had on, and laid out the bodies upon the bed. They then went to call Sir James Tyrrel, who was all ready, in an apartment not far off, awaiting the summons. He came at once, and, when he saw that the boys were really dead, he gave orders that the men should take the bodies down into the court-yard to be buried.

The burial.

The grave was dug immediately, just outside the door, at the foot of the stairs which led up to the turret in which the boys had been confined. When the bodies had been placed in the ground, the grave was filled up, and some stones were put upon the top of it.

Immediately after this work had been accomplished, Sir James delivered back the keys to the governor of the castle, and mounted his horse to return to the king. He traveled with all possible speed, and, on reaching the place where the king then was, he reported what he had done.

Joy of Richard.

The king was extremely pleased, and he rewarded Sir James very liberally for his energy and zeal; he, however, expressed some dissatisfaction at the manner in which the bodies had been disposed of. "They should not have been buried," he said, "in so vile a corner."

Re-interment of the bodies.

So Richard sent word to the governor of the Tower, and the governor commissioned a priest to take up the bodies secretly, and inter them again in a more suitable manner. This priest soon afterward died, without revealing the place which he chose for the interment, and so it was never known where the bodies were finally laid.

Richard keeps the murder secret.

Richard gave all the persons who had been concerned in this affair very strict instructions to keep the death of the princes a profound secret. He did not intend to make it known, unless he should perceive some indication of an attempt to restore Edward to the throne; and, had it not been for the occurrence of certain circumstances which will be related in the next chapter, the fate of the princes might, perhaps, have thus been kept secret for many years.

Chapter XVI
Domestic Troubles

A.D. 1483-1484

Plots formed against Richard.

While Richard was making his triumphal tour through the north of England, apparently receiving a confirmation of his right to the crown by the voice of the whole population of the country, the leaders of the Lancaster party were secretly beginning, in London, to form their schemes for liberating the young princes from the Tower, and restoring Edward to the kingdom.

Situation of Elizabeth Woodville.

Queen Elizabeth, who still remained, with the Princess Elizabeth, her oldest daughter, and some of her other children, in the sanctuary at Westminster, was the centre of this movement. She communicated privately with the nobles who were disposed to espouse her cause. The nobles had secret meetings among themselves to form their plans. At these meetings they drank to the health of the king in the Tower, and of his brother, the little Duke of York, and pledged themselves to do every thing in their power to restore the king to his throne. They little knew that the unhappy princes were at that very time lying together in a corner of the court-yard of the prison in an ignoble grave.

Plans of the conspirators.
Queen Elizabeth's agony.

At length the conspirators' plans were matured, and the insurrection broke out. Richard immediately prepared to leave York, at the head of a strong force, to go toward London. At the same time, he allowed the tidings to be spread abroad that the two princes were dead. This news greatly disconcerted the conspirators and deranged their plans; and when the dreadful intelligence was communicated to the queen in the sanctuary, she was stunned, and almost killed by it, as by a blow. "She swooned away, and fell to the ground, where she lay in great agony, like a corpse;" and when at length she was restored to consciousness again, she broke forth in shrieks and cries of anguish so loud, that they resounded through the whole Abbey, and were most pitiful to hear. She beat her breast and tore her hair, calling all the time to her children by their names, and bitterly reproaching herself for her madness in giving up the youngest into his enemies' hands. After exhausting herself with these cries and lamentations, she sank into a state of calm despair, and, kneeling down upon the floor, she began, with dreadful earnestness and solemnity, to call upon Almighty God, imploring him to avenge the death of her children, and invoking the bitterest curses upon the head of their ruthless murderer.

QUEEN ELIZABETH AT THE GRAVE OF HER CHILDREN

Retribution.

It was but a short time after this that Richard's child died at Middleham Castle, as stated in the last chapter. Many persons believed that this calamity was a judgment of heaven, brought upon the king in answer to the bereaved mother's imprecations.

Elizabeth visits the grave.

It is said that when Queen Elizabeth had recovered a little from the first shock of her grief, she demanded to be taken to her children's grave. So they conducted her to the Tower, and showed her the place in the corner of the court-yard where they had first been buried.

The Duke of Buckingham.

One of the principal leaders of the conspiracy which had been

152

formed against Richard was the Duke of Buckingham—the same that had taken so active a part in bringing Richard to the throne. What induced him to change sides so suddenly is not certainly known. It is supposed that he was dissatisfied with the rewards which Richard bestowed upon him. At any rate, he now turned against the king, and became the leader of the conspirators that were plotting against him.

Richmond.
Elizabeth.
Plans formed for a marriage.

When the conspirators heard of the death of the princes, they were at first at a loss to know what to do. They looked about among the branches of the York and Lancaster families for some one to make their candidate for the crown. At last they decided upon a certain Henry Tudor, Earl of Richmond. This Henry, or Richmond, as he was generally called, was descended indirectly from the Lancaster line. The proposal of the conspirators, however, was, that he should marry the Princess Elizabeth, Queen Elizabeth Woodville's daughter, who has already been mentioned among those who fled with their mother to the sanctuary. Now that both the sons of Elizabeth were dead, this daughter was, of course, King Edward's next heir, and by her marriage with Richmond the claims of the houses of York and Lancaster would be, in a measure, combined.

When this plan was proposed to Queen Elizabeth, she acceded to it at once, and promised that she would give her daughter in marriage to Richmond, and acknowledge him as king, provided he would first conquer and depose King Richard, the common enemy.

Richmond plans an invasion.

The plan was accordingly all arranged. Richmond was in France at this time, having fled there some time previous, after a battle, in which his party had been defeated. They wrote to him, explaining the plan. He immediately fell in with it. He raised a small force—all that he could procure at that time—and set sail, with a few ships, from the port of St. Malo, intending to land on the coast of Devonshire, which is in the southwestern part of England.

In the mean time, the several leaders of the rebellion had gone to different parts of the kingdom, in order to raise troops, and form centres of action against Richard. Buckingham went into Wales. His plan was to march down, with all the forces that he could raise there, to the coast of Devonshire, to meet Richmond on his landing.

This Richard resolved to prevent. He raised an army, and marched to intercept Buckingham. He first, however, issued a proclamation in which he denounced the leaders of the rebellion as criminals and outlaws, and set a price upon their heads.

Buckingham's attempt to co-operate.
Failure of the plan.
Death of Buckingham.

Buckingham did not succeed in reaching the coast in time to join Richmond. He was stopped by the River Severn, which you will see, by looking on a map of England, came directly in his way. He tried to get across the river, but the people destroyed the bridges and the boats, and he could not get over. He marched up to where the stream was small, in hopes of finding a fording place, but the waters were so swollen with the fall rains that he failed in this attempt as well as the others. The result was, that Richard came up while Buckingham was entangled among the intricacies of the ground produced by the inundations. Buckingham's soldiers, seeing that they were likely to be surrounded, abandoned him and fled. At last Buckingham fled too, and hid himself; but one of his servants came and told Richard where he was. Richard ordered him to be seized. Buckingham sent an imploring message to Richard, begging that Richard would see him, and, before condemning him, hear what he had to say; but Richard, in the place of any reply, gave orders to the soldiers to take the prisoner at once out into the public square of the town, and cut off his head. The order was immediately obeyed.

Richmond retreats.

When Richmond reached the coast of Devonshire, and found that Buckingham was not there to meet him, he was afraid to land with the small force that he had under his command, and so he sailed back to France.

Thus the first attempt made to organize a forcible resistance to Richard's power totally failed.

Unhappy situation of Elizabeth.

The unhappy queen, when she heard these tidings, was once more overwhelmed with grief. Her situation in the sanctuary was becoming every day more and more painful. She had long since exhausted all her own means, and she imagined that the monks began to think that she was availing herself of their hospitality too long. Her friends without would gladly have supplied her wants, but this Richard would not permit. He set a guard around the sanctuary, and would not allow any one to come or go. He would starve her out, he said, if he could not compel her to surrender herself in any other way.

The princess.

It was, however, not the queen herself, but her daughter Elizabeth, who was now the heir of whatever claims to the throne were possessed by the family, that Richard was most anxious to secure. If he could once get Elizabeth into his power, he thought, he could easily devise some plan to prevent her marriage with Henry of Richmond, and so defeat the plans of his enemies in the most effectual manner. He would have liked still better to have secured Henry himself; but Henry was in Brittany, on the other side of the Channel, beyond his reach.

He seeks to get possession of Richmond.

He, however, formed a secret plan to get possession of Henry. He offered privately a large reward to the Duke of Brittany if he would seize Henry and deliver him into his, Richard's hands. This the duke engaged to do. But Henry gained intelligence of the plot before it was executed, and made his escape from Brittany into France. He was received kindly at Paris by the French king. The king even promised to aid him in deposing Richard, and making himself King of England instead. This alarmed Richard more than ever.

Parliament.

In the mean time, the summer passed away and the autumn came on. In November Richard convened Parliament, and caused very severe laws to be passed against those who had been engaged in the rebellion. Many were executed under these laws, some were banished, and others shut up in prison. Richard attempted, by these and similar measures, to break down the spirit of his enemies, and prevent the possibility of their forming any new organizations against him. Still, notwithstanding all that he could do, he felt very ill at ease so long as Henry and Elizabeth were at liberty.

New policy.

At last, in the course of the winter, he conceived the idea of trying what pretended kindness could do in enticing the queen and her family out of sanctuary. So he sent a messenger to her, to make fair and friendly proposals to her in case she would give up her place of refuge and place herself under his protection. He said that he felt no animosity or ill will against her, but that, if she and her daughters would trust to him, he would receive them at court, provide for them fully in a manner suited to their rank, and treat them in all respects with the highest consideration. She herself should be recognized as the queen dowager of England, and her daughters as princesses of the royal family; and he would take proper measures to arrange marriages for the young ladies, such as should comport with the exalted station which they were entitled to hold.

The plan succeeds.
Excuses for the queen.

The queen was at last persuaded to yield to these solicitations. She left the sanctuary, and gave herself and her daughters up to Richard's control. Many persons have censured her very strongly for doing this; but her friends and defenders allege that there was nothing else that she could do. She might have remained in the Abbey herself to starve if she had been alone, but she could not see her children perish of destitution and distress when a word from her could restore them to the world, and raise them at once to a condition of the highest prosperity and honor. So she yielded. She left the Abbey, and was established by Richard in one of his palaces, and her daughters were received at court, and treated, especially the eldest, with the utmost consideration.

Her situation still unhappy.

But, notwithstanding this outward change in her condition, the real situation of the queen herself, after leaving the Abbey, was extremely forlorn. The apartments which Richard assigned to her were very retired and obscure. He required her, moreover, to dismiss all her own attendants, and he appointed servants and agents of his own to wait upon and guard her. The queen soon found that she was under a very strict surveillance, and not much less a prisoner, in fact, than she was before.

The marriage countermanded.

While in this situation, she wrote to her son Dorset, [10] at Paris, commanding him to put an end to the proposed marriage of her daughter Elizabeth to Henry of Richmond, "as she had given up," she said, "the plan of that alliance, and had formed other designs for the princess." Henry and his friends and partisans in Paris were indignant at receiving this letter, and the queen has been by many persons much blamed for having thus broken the engagement which she had so solemnly made. Others say that this letter to Paris was not her free act, but that it was extorted from her by Richard, who had her now completely in his power, and could, of course, easily find means to procure from her any writing that he might desire.

Whether the queen acted freely or not in this case can not certainly be known. At all events, Henry, and those who were acting with him at Paris, determined to regard the letter as written under constraint, and to go on with the maturing of their plans just as if it had never been written.

Richard's plan for the princess.
Elizabeth's views on the subject.

Richard's plan was, so it was said, to marry the Princess Elizabeth to his own son; for the death of his child, though it has been already once or twice alluded to, had not yet taken place. Richard's son was very young, being at that time about eleven years old; but the princess might be affianced to him, and the marriage consummated when he grew up. Elizabeth herself seems to have fallen in with this proposed arrangement very readily. The prospect that Henry of Richmond would ever succeed in making himself king, and claiming her for his bride, was very remote and uncertain, while Richard was already in full possession of power; and she, by taking his side, and becoming the affianced wife of his son, became at once the first lady in the kingdom, next to Queen Anne, with an apparently certain prospect of becoming queen herself in due time.

Death of Richard's son.

But all these fine plans were abruptly brought to an end by the death of the young prince, which occurred about this time, at

---

[10] The Earl of Dorset, you will recollect, was Queen Elizabeth's son by her first marriage; he, consequently, had no claim to the crown.

Middleham Castle, as has been stated before. The death of the poor boy took place in a very sudden and mysterious manner. Some persons supposed that he died by a judgment from heaven, in answer to the awful curses which Queen Elizabeth Woodville imprecated upon the head of the murderer of her children; others thought he was destroyed by poison.

Sickness of Queen Anne.
Sufferings of the queen.

Not very long after the death of the prince, his mother fell very seriously sick. She was broken-hearted at the death of her son, and pining away, she fell into a slow decline. Her sufferings were greatly aggravated by Richard's harsh and cruel treatment of her. He was continually uttering expressions of impatience against her on account of her sickness and uselessness, and making fretful complaints of her various disagreeable qualities. Some of these sayings were reported to Anne, and also a rumor came to her ears one day, while she was at her toilet, that Richard was intending to put her to death. She was dreadfully alarmed at hearing this, and she immediately ran, half dressed as she was, and with her hair disheveled, into the presence of her husband, and, with piteous sobs and bitter tears, asked him what she had done to deserve death. Richard tried to quiet and calm her, assuring her that she had no cause to fear.

Suspicions.

She, however, continued to decline; and not long afterward her distress and anguish of mind were greatly increased by hearing that Richard was impatient for her death, in order that he might himself marry the Princess Elizabeth, to whom every one said he was now, since the death of his son, devoting himself personally with great attention. In this state of suffering the poor queen lingered on through the months of the winter, very evidently, though slowly, approaching her end. The universal belief was that Richard had formed the plan of making the Princess Elizabeth his wife, and that the decline and subsequent death of Anne were owing to a slow poison which he caused to be administered to her. There is no proof that this charge was true, but the general belief in the truth of it shows what was the estimate placed, in those times, on Richard's character.

Elizabeth's eagerness to marry the king.

It is very certain, however, that he contemplated this new marriage, and that the princess herself acceded to the proposed plan, and was very deeply interested in the accomplishment of it. It is said that while the queen still lived she wrote to one of her friends—a certain noble duke of high standing and influence—in which she implored him to aid in forwarding her marriage with the king, whom she called "her master and her joy in this world—the master of her heart and thoughts." In this letter, too, she expressed her impatience at the queen's being so long in dying. "Only think," said she, "the better part of February is past, and the queen is still alive. Will she *never* die?"

Death of the queen.

But the patience of the princess was not destined to be taxed much longer. The queen sank rapidly after this, and in March she died.

The heart of Elizabeth was now filled with exultation and delight. The great obstacle to her marriage with her uncle was now removed, and the way was open before her to become a queen. It is true that the relationship which existed between her and Richard, that of uncle and niece, was such as to make the marriage utterly illegal. But Richard had a plan of obtaining a dispensation from the Pope, which he had no doubt that he could easily do, and a dispensation from the Pope, according to the ideas of those times, would legalize any thing. So Richard cautiously proposed his plan to some of his confidential counselors.

Remonstrance of Richard's counselors.

His counselors told him that the execution of such a plan would be dangerous in the highest degree. The people of England, they said, had for some time been led to think that the king had that design in contemplation, and that the idea had awakened a great deal of indignation throughout the country. The land was full of rumors and murmurings, they said, and those of a very threatening character. The marriage would be considered incestuous both by the clergy and the people, and would be looked upon with abhorrence. Besides, they said, there were a great many dark suspicions in the minds of the people that Richard had been himself the cause of the death of his former wife Anne, in order to open the way for this marriage, and now, if the marriage were really to take place, all these suspicions would be confirmed. They could judge somewhat, they added, by the depth of the excitement which had been produced by the bare suspicion that such things were contemplated, how great would be the violence of the outbreak of public indignation if the design were carried into effect. Richard would be in the utmost danger of losing his kingdom.

PORTRAIT OF THE PRINCESS ELIZABETH

Richard gives up the plan.

So Richard determined at once to abandon the plan. He caused it to be announced in the most public manner that he had never contemplated such a marriage, and that all the rumors attributing such a design to him were malicious and false. He also sent orders abroad throughout the kingdom requiring that all persons who had circulated such rumors should be arrested and sent to London to be punished.

Disappointment of Elizabeth.

Elizabeth's hopes were, of course, suddenly blasted, and the splendid castle which her imagination had built fell to the ground. It was only a temporary disappointment, however, for she became Queen of England in the end, after all.

Richmond goes on with his preparations at Paris.

In the mean time, while Richard had been occupied with the schemes and manoeuvres described in the last chapter, Richmond was going on steadily in Paris with the preparations that he was making for a new invasion of England. The King of France assisted him both by providing him with money and aiding him in the enlistment of men. When Richmond received the message from Elizabeth's mother declaring that the proposed match between him and the princess must be broken off, and heard that Richard had formed a plan for marrying the young lady himself, he paid no regard to the tidings, but declared that he should proceed with his plans as vigorously as ever, and that, whatever counter-schemes they might form, they might rely upon it that he should fully carry into effect his purpose, not only of deposing Richard and reigning in his stead, but also of making the Princess Elizabeth his wife, according to his original intention.

The expedition sails.

At length the expedition was ready, and the fleet conveying it set sail from the port of Harfleur.

Richard issues a proclamation.

Richard attempted to arouse the people of England against the invaders by a grand proclamation which he issued. In this proclamation he designated the Earl of Richmond as "one Henry Tudor," who had no claim whatever, of any kind, to the English throne, but who was coming to attempt to seize it without any color of right. In order to obtain assistance from the King of France, he had promised, the proclamation said, "to surrender to him, in case he was successful, all the rich possessions in France which at that time belonged to England, even Calais itself; and he had promised, moreover, and given away, to the traitors and foreigners who were coming with him, all the most important and valuable places in the kingdom—archbishoprics, bishoprics, duchies, earldoms, baronies, and many other inheritances belonging of right to the English knights, esquires, and gentlemen who were now in the possession of them. The proclamation farther declared that the people who made up his army were robbers and murderers, and rebels attainted by Parliament, many of whom had made themselves infamous as cutthroats, adulterers, and extortioners."

Richard closed his proclamation by calling upon all his subjects to arm themselves, like true and good Englishmen, for the defense of their wives, children, goods, and hereditaments, and he promised that he himself, like a true and courageous prince, would put himself in the forefront of the battle, and expose his royal person to the worst of the dangers that were to be incurred in the defense of the country.

Plans of the campaign.
The king goes to Nottingham.

At the same time that he issued this proclamation, Richard sent forth orders to all parts of the kingdom, commanding the nobles and barons to marshal their forces, and make ready to march at a moment's warning. He dispatched detachments of his forces to the southward to defend the southern coast, where he expected Richmond would land, while he himself proceeded northward, toward the centre of the kingdom, to assemble and organize his grand army. He made Nottingham his head-quarters, and he gradually gathered around him, in that city, a very large force.

In the mean time, while these movements and preparations had been going on on both sides, the spring and the early part of the summer passed away, and at length Richard, at Nottingham, in the month of August, received the tidings that Richmond had landed at Milford Haven, on the southwestern coast of Wales, with a force of two or three thousand men. Richard said that he was glad to hear it. "I am glad," said he, "that at last he has come. I have now only to meet him, and gain one decisive victory, and then the security of my kingdom will be disturbed no more."

Richmond's hopes and expectations.
The various negotiations.

Richmond did not rely wholly on the troops which he had brought with him for the success of his cause. He believed that there was a great and prevailing feeling of disaffection against Richard throughout England, and that, as soon as it should appear that he, Richmond, was really in earnest in his determination to claim and take the crown, and that there was a reasonable prospect of the success of his enterprise, great numbers of men, who were now ostensibly on Richard's side, would forsake him and join the invader. So he sent secret messengers throughout the kingdom to communicate with his friends, and to open negotiations with those of Richard's adherents who might possibly be inclined to change sides. In order to give time for these negotiations to produce their effect, he resolved not to march at once into the interior of the country, but to proceed slowly toward the eastward, along the southern coast of Wales, awaiting intelligence. This plan he pursued. His strength increased rapidly as he advanced. At length, when he reached the eastern borders of Wales, he began to feel strong enough to push forward into England to meet Richard, who was all this time gathering his forces together at Nottingham, and preparing for a very formidable resistance of the invader. He accordingly advanced to Leicester, and thence to the town of Tamworth, where there was a strong castle on a rock. He took possession of this castle, and made it, for a time, his head-quarters.

Richard at Nottingham.
He commences his march.

In the mean time, Richard, having received intelligence of Richmond's movements, and having now made every thing ready for his own advance, determined to delay no longer, but to go forth and meet his enemy. Accordingly, one morning, he marshaled his troops in the market-place of Nottingham, "separating his foot-soldiers in two divisions, five abreast, and dividing his cavalry so as to form two wide-spreading wings." He placed his artillery, with the ammunition, in the centre, reserving for himself a position in a space immediately behind it.

The long column.

When all was ready, he came out from the castle mounted upon a milk-white charger. He wore, according to the custom of the times, a very magnificent armor, resplendent with gold and embroidery, and with polished steel that glittered in the sun. Over his helmet he wore his royal crown. He was preceded and followed, as he came out through the castle gates and descended the winding way which led down from the hill on which the castle stands, by guards splendidly dressed and mounted—archers, and spearmen, and other men at arms—with ensigns bearing innumerable pennants and banners. As soon as he joined the army in the town the order was given to march, and so great was the number of men that he had under his command that they were more than an hour in marching out of Nottingham, and when all had finally issued from the gate, the column covered the road for three miles.

Bosworth.

At length, after some days of manoeuvring and marching, the two armies came into the immediate vicinity of each other near the town of Bosworth, at a place where there was a wide field, which has since been greatly renowned in history as the Field of Bosworth. The two armies advanced into the neighborhood of this field on the 19th and 20th days of August, and both sides began to prepare for battle.

The two armies.
Richard's depression and anxiety.
His painful suspicions.

The army which Richard commanded was far more numerous and imposing than that of Richmond, and every thing, so far as outward appearances were concerned, promised him an easy victory. And yet Richmond was exultant in his confidence of success, while Richard was harassed with gloomy forebodings. His mind was filled with perplexity and distress. He believed that the leading nobles and generals on his side had secretly resolved to betray him, and that they were prepared to abandon him and go over to the enemy on the very field of battle, unless he could gain advantages so decisive at the very commencement of the conflict as to show that the cause of Richmond was hopeless. Although Richard was morally convinced that this was the state of things, he had no sufficient evidence of it to justify his taking any action against the men that he suspected. He did not even dare to express his suspicions, for he knew that if he were to do so, or even to intimate that he felt suspicion, the only effect would be to precipitate the consummation of the treachery that he feared, and perhaps drive some to abandon him who had not yet fully resolved on doing so. He was obliged, therefore, though suffering the greatest anxiety and alarm, to suppress all indications of his uneasiness, except to his most confidential friends. To them he appeared, as one of them stated, "sore moved and broiled with melancholy and dolor, and from time to time he cried out, asking vengeance of them that, contrary to their oath and promise, were so deceiving him."

His remorse.

The recollection of the many crimes that he had committed in the attainment of the power which he now feared he was about to lose forever, harassed his mind and tormented his conscience, especially at night. "He took ill rest at nights," says one of his biographers, "using to lie long, waking and musing, sore wearied with care and watch, and rather slumbered than slept, troubled with fearful dreams."

The battle.
Richard betrayed.
Defection of his men.

On the day of the battle Richard found the worst of his forebodings fulfilled. In the early part of the day he took a position upon an elevated portion of the ground, where he could survey the whole field, and direct the movements of his troops. From this point he could see, as the battle went on, one body of men after another go over to the enemy. He was overwhelmed with vexation and rage. He cried out, Treason! Treason! and, calling upon his guards and attendants to follow him, he rushed down the hill, determined to force his way to the part of the field where Richmond himself was stationed, with a view of engaging him and killing him with his own hand. This, he thought, was the last hope that was now left him.

There was a spring of water, and a little brook flowing from it in a part of the field where he had to pass. He stopped at this spring, opened his helmet, and took a drink of the water. He then closed his helmet and rode on.

Richard's Well.

This spring afterward received, from this circumstance, the name of "Richard's Well," and it is known by that name to this day.

His despair.
Terrible combat.

From the spring Richard rushed forward, attended by a few followers as fearless as himself, in search of Richmond. He penetrated the enemies' lines in the direction where he supposed Richmond was to be found, and was soon surrounded by foes, whom he engaged desperately in a hand-to-hand encounter of the most furious and reckless character. He slew one or two of the foremost of those who surrounded him, calling out all the time to Richmond to come out and meet him in single combat. This Richmond would not do. In the mean time, many of Richard's friends came up to his assistance. Some of these urged him to retire, saying that it was useless for him to attempt to maintain so unequal a contest, but he refused to go.

He refuses to fly.

"Not one foot will I fly," said he, "so long as breath bides within my breast; for, by Him that shaped both sea and land, this day shall end my battles or my life. I will die King of England."

So he fought on. Several faithful friends still adhered to him and fought by his side. His standard-bearer stood his ground, with the king's banner in his hand, until at last both his legs were cut off under him, and he fell to the earth; still he would not let the banner go, but clung to it with a convulsive grasp till he died.

Richard is killed.

At last Richard too was overpowered by the numbers that beset him. Exhausted by his exertions, and weakened by loss of blood, he was beaten down from his horse to the ground and killed. The royal crown which he had worn so proudly into the battle was knocked from his head in the dreadful affray, and trampled in the dust.

Transfer of the crown.

Lord Stanley, one of the chieftains who had abandoned Richard's cause and gone over to the enemy, picked up the crown, all battered and bloodstained as it was, and put it upon Richmond's head. From that hour Richmond was recognized as King of England. He reigned under the title of Henry the Seventh.

KING HENRY VII

Flight of Richard's troops.
Disposition of the body.

The few followers that had remained faithful to Richard's cause up to this time now gave up the contest and fled. The victors lifted up the dead body of the king, took off the armor, and then placed the body across the back of a horse, behind a pursuivant-at-arms, who, thus mounted, rode a little behind the new king as he retired from the field of battle. Followed by this dreadful trophy of his victory, King Henry entered the town of Leicester in triumph. The body of Richard was exposed for three days, in a public place, to the view of all beholders, in order that every body might be satisfied that he was really dead, and then the new king proceeded by easy journeys to London. The people came out to meet him all along the way, receiving him every where with shouts and acclamations, and crying, "King Henry! King Henry! Long live our sovereign lord, King Henry!"

Henry marries the princess.

For several weeks after his accession Henry's mind was occupied with public affairs, but, as soon as the most urgent of the calls upon his attention were disposed of, he renewed his proposals to the Princess Elizabeth, and in January of the next year they were married. It seems to have been a matter of no consequence to her whether one man or another was her husband, provided he was only King of England, so that she could be queen. Henry's motive, too, in marrying her, was equally mercenary, his only object being to secure to himself, through her, the right of inheritance to her father's claims to the throne. He accordingly never pretended to feel any love for her, and, after his marriage, he treated her with great coldness and neglect.

Queen Elizabeth Woodville.
Last years of her life.

His conduct toward her poor mother, the dowager queen, Elizabeth Woodville, was still more unfriendly. He sent her to a gloomy monastery, called the Monastery of Bermondsey, and caused her to be kept there in the custody of the monks, virtually a prisoner. The reason which he assigned for this was his displeasure with her for abandoning his cause, and breaking the engagement which she had made with him for the marriage of her daughter to him, and also for giving herself and her daughter up into Richard's hands, and joining with him in the intrigues which Richard formed for connecting the princess with his family. In this lonely retreat the widowed queen passed the remainder of her days. She was not precisely a prisoner—at least, she was not kept in close and continual confinement, for two or three times, in the course of the few remaining years that she lived, she was brought, on special occasions, to court, and treated there with a certain degree of attention and respect. One of these occasions was that of the baptism of her daughter's child.

THE MONASTERY OF BERMONDSEY

Her death and burial.

In this lonely and cheerless retreat the queen lingered a few years, and then died. Her body was conveyed to Windsor for interment, and her daughters and the friends of her family were notified of the event. A very few came to attend the funeral. Her daughter Elizabeth was indisposed, and did not come. The interment took place at night. A few poor old men, in tattered garments, were employed to officiate at the ceremony by holding "old torches and torches' ends" to light the gloomy precincts of the chapel during the time while the monks were chanting the funeral dirge.

The End